COOKING FOR BLOKES

COOKING
FOR
BLOKES

Duncan Anderson & Marian Walls

WARNER BOOKS

A *Warner* Book

First published in Great Britain in 1996 by Warner Books
Reprinted 1996 (four times), 1997 (twice), 1998 (three times),
1999 (twice), 2000 (twice), 2001

A CIP catalogue record for this book
is available from the British Library.

ISBN 0 7515 1563 9

Typeset by Solidus (Bristol) Limited
Printed and bound in Great Britain by
Clays Ltd, St Ives plc

Warner Books
A Division of
Little, Brown and Company (UK)
Brettenham House
Lancaster Place
London WC2E 7EN

www.littlebrown.co.uk

CONTENTS

Introduction	1
How hot is your oven?	4
Tools	6
Get a cupboard	15
How to ...	17
Starters	30
Snacks	47
Salads & Dressings	61
Eggs	87
Chicken	100
Fish	118
Meat	141
Vegetarian	174
Desserts	194
Chinese & Far Eastern	222
Italian	240
Tex-Mex	270
Indian	290
Parties	312
Drinks	315
Index	321

INTRODUCTION

The First Rule of this book is don't panic.

We hope all the instructions are clear and simple and the recipes are easy to follow. You don't need to know anything about cooking to use this book and it is good to remember that there is nothing mysterious about cooking. It is not some religious discipline requiring years of study, a funny haircut, a massive kitchen, thousands of spoons, a working knowledge of French, or an account at your local speciality food emporium. Millions of people have been doing it for years and most have survived.

If someone has bought you this book then you are probably going to have to make one of our recipes. We have included recipes which don't need any cooking at all, so if you are at all nervous about cooking, this may be a good place to start. Each chapter is graded with the easier recipes at the front and the more difficult ones last. None is really difficult, and all of them will taste good and look good.

All of the recipes are flexible and forgiving. You do not need to be obsessional about getting the exact amount of an ingredient to the nearest gram. Lots of the ingredients come in packs, tins or tubs in standard sizes. Recipes take advantage of this. Some use half a standard pack, for instance for dried pasta. With meat and fish just ask for the amount you want at the shop, or look for a pack of about the same size. We have tried to suggest quantities that won't cause a lot of waste, but sometimes it has been impossible to use a whole can or jar or packet in a recipe. You may have left-overs of cooked foods too. We have tried to use some of these in other recipes.

Cooking for yourself means you can take control of what you eat, and it won't be money that makes you decide between Mexican and Indian or a pizza, it'll be your taste buds. Think about it. You can eat what you like. I like Mexican food. I can go to a restaurant and get some over-priced beer and tortillas which may be either too hot or not hot enough, or I can have a go at it myself. OK, the first time I try it may be too hot or not hot enough, but the next time it will be better.

It's a lot cheaper to cook for yourself than live on take-aways, oven-ready meals or eating out in restaurants. I had a friend who over the years gradually made more money, but was always broke. Whenever he needed to eat, it was corn flakes, muesli or toast, or something bought. A bought sandwich, a take-away. He had a series of girlfriends that he was trying to impress and they couldn't cook either. Restaurants every night can lead to financial ruin, and he couldn't drink because he had to drive, so he spent his life deciding which take-away to go to.

Is cooking easy? Yes.
Does it save you money? Yes.
Does it give you control over what you eat? Yes.
Is it an impressive thing to be able to do? We think so.
Is it enjoyable? 95% of the time.

We have tried to think of everything you would need to know to start cooking easy and exciting recipes.

Just like any other activity you need a few tools to get started. There is a section on tools you will need, and some you don't need but might like because they make some things that much easier. You may need an electric drill to put up shelves but you only need a knife and a couple of pans and a set of measuring spoons to get started cooking.

You don't need a set of scales; instead, wherever possible, we use spoons and cups for measuring. There are standard measuring spoons and cups that come in sets in plastic or metal. Those you eat and drink from may not be standard.

In case you decide to brave it without even the measuring cups or spoons, a measuring cup is about the same size as a half-pint (250 ml) mug. There are a bunch of recipes where you won't even need the spoons or cups.

There is a 'How to ...' section which deals with general things like cooking vegetables, rice and pasta. Defrosting has a small space to itself because you will probably find frozen food reasonably priced and convenient if you shop for more than a day at a time.

There's a list of basic cheap food items you could think of keeping for stand-by.

Recipes are grouped together. We have started with starters and snacks, and then some grouped by food type: eggs, chicken, fish, meat, vegetarian and desserts. The second part takes food from the take-away and restaurant. Chinese stir-fry and satay, Italian pasta and pizza, Tex-Mex ribs, tacos, sauces and beans, Indian curries and sauces, parties and drinks.

Give it a go.

HOW HOT IS YOUR OVEN?

Ovens and temperatures

Every recipe that needs an oven has got the correct cooking time and oven temperature in the recipe. We have gathered all the temperatures from various cookers here. Approximate equivalent temperatures are shown below for different ovens.

140°C, 275°F, Gas mark 1
150°C, 300°F, Gas mark 2
170°C, 325°F, Gas mark 3
180°C, 350°F, Gas mark 4
190°C, 375°F, Gas mark 5
200°C, 400°F, Gas mark 6
220°C, 425°F, Gas mark 7
230°C, 450°F, Gas mark 8
240°C, 475°F, Gas mark 9

Gas ovens and fan-assisted ovens get hotter quicker than standard electric ones.

In most ovens the top is hotter than the bottom. Most things are best cooked in the middle. Roast potatoes and vegetables are best cooked at the top if you like them crispy.

Fan-assisted ovens have less of a difference between top and bottom and need different cooking times. Please refer to your instruction book.

Microwave cooker

There are no recipes for microwave cookers in this book. Please write to the publisher and demand the commissioning of a slim companion volume, 'Cooking for Blokes (the Microwave Years)'.

TOOLS

THE BASICS

In this book all the tools you need for a particular recipe are listed after the ingredients. The information in this chapter should help you decide which are the most suitable for you.

Sharp knives

Knives are the most important tools. They must be sharp. They do not need sharpening every day or even every week, but they will eventually get blunt. Just like some tools are better than others, and generally more expensive, so it is with knives. Within reason, more expensive knives last longer and keep an edge longer.

If you only buy one knife choose a 'kitchen knife'. The blade should be about 16 to 20 cm (6½ to 8 inches) long with a comfortable handle. It should have a gently curved edge. It should have a smooth chopping blade rather than be serrated. This size and kind of knife can be used for chopping vegetables and meat as well as carving.

The next most important kind is a small knife for cutting up smaller things. This can double as a vegetable peeler. The blade should be about 10 cm (4 inches) long.

Knife sharpeners

Buy a cheap one and follow the instructions.

One kind looks like crossed fingers. You pull the knife through a few times and it puts an edge on both sides of the knife at the same time.

'Butcher's steels' (the long pointed sharpeners with a handle) need a lot of practice to use properly and can lead to injury in the overconfident starter.

Electric sharpeners, like a lot of time-saving ideas, are an expensive waste of space.

Chopping boards

These should be made of plastic.

A plain round wooden board is all right for cutting bread on, but unhygienic for meat, fish or vegetables.

Basic hygiene and the state of some food (remember salmonella in eggs and chickens) gives two rules for using chopping boards. First, keep them clean. Wash them every time you use them. Second, chop the vegetables, salad or cheese before chopping any meat or fish. This is because the salad may get infected with bugs from the meat. The bugs are killed by cooking.

Measuring spoons & cups

Recipes in this book use spoonfuls or cupfuls rather than weights for most things. If you look in any kitchen you will see that teaspoons and cups come in several sizes. This means the amounts and so the taste may be very different if you just use any cup or spoon. To get round this problem, buy a set of spoons and cups in standard sizes. Look in the cooking section of your local supermarket. They come in plastic or stainless steel.

> One teaspoonful is 5 ml.
> One tablespoonful is 15 ml.

The cup set looks like a very large spoon set, and has four sizes:

1 cup	250 ml	approx. 9 fluid ounces
Half a cup	125 ml	4 fl oz
Third of a cup	80 ml	3 fl oz
Quarter cup	60 ml	2 fl oz

This makes from some easy conversions. A pint is 20 fl oz, and is approximately two and a quarter cups.

Some cups are based on 240 ml to the cup. Either sort will do. The difference between them is only about five per cent and well within the tolerance of the recipes.

Wooden spoons, spatulas and other spoons

Minimum requirements are a wooden spoon and a spatula (it gets into the corners better).

Next most important is a cooking spoon for getting stuff out of pans and on to plates.

Next is a fish slice and a spoon with holes in it for draining.

If you buy a set, make sure it is not going to melt if it gets warm or scratch your nice aluminium non-stick pans.

Bowls

You need bowls to mix things in. If the bowl looks OK you can use it to serve food in as well. Choose a plastic or glass one and make sure it is big enough.

Vegetable peelers

A small sharp knife will do, but there are some specially made vegetable peelers which are slightly safer and easier to use.

One is a bit like a knife and sometimes has an apple corer at the end furthest from the handle.

Another looks a bit like a letter D with the straight edge of the D being a slotted blade.

Pans – overall advice

Buy a cheap set and then go looking in street markets or car boot sales for second-hand cast-iron pans with enamelled insides. This is where being a bloke will be an advantage. People buy these and then decide they don't like using them because they are too heavy. You, on the other hand, will have no trouble with them.

The cheapest sets are aluminium non-stick.

Saucepans

Buy pans with lids.

How many?
At least one and preferably two.

What size?

22 cm (8½ inches) across. 2 litres (3½ pints). This is big enough to cook pasta or rice or stew.

16 cm (6½ inches) across. 1 litre (1¾ pints). This is big enough for tomato sauce for pasta, custard or frozen peas.

Stick or non-stick?

Go for non-stick. Most aluminium pans have a non-stick coating. But remember, this is easy to remove with forks, metal implements and scouring pads. It can also make an interesting chemical burning smell if you heat it up too much with nothing in the pan, which may put you off eating for some time.

What metal?

Aluminium: The cheap ones will wear out in a couple of years. By this time you will have decided if you want to continue to cook and whether to keep buying cheap ones or go for something better.

Stainless steel: Very shiny. Quite expensive. Longer lasting. Thicker bases distribute the heat more evenly. This means that if you forget to stir, the food sticks evenly to the bottom of the pan rather than in the shape of the heating element. Thinner bases mean more stirring. Stainless steel saucepans can be soaked in hot soapy water and burnt-on food will come away fairly easily.

Cast iron with enamel interior (eg Le Creuset): These are expensive, very durable and heavy. They cook very evenly. The enamel lining makes them practically non-stick. They do not like being heated up with nothing in them and the enamel may crack if you move them too quickly from heat to cold water. They can be soaked in water but the wooden handles don't like it. The handles can char if you cook on too high gas. Handles and casserole lids can be bought separately and replaced.

Frying-pans

General advice as to sort of metal is as above.

Size should be about 25 to 28 cm (10 to 11 inches across).

If you want to cook a lot of omelettes buy a smaller one as well, say 20 cm (8 inches).

Casserole with lid

There are three sorts: pottery, ovenproof glass or cast iron. These are used for cooking in the oven. Cooking this way is an easy option because you can just put the food in the oven and leave it to cook while you do something else.

If you go and look in a shop you will see some ovenproof glass (Pyrex type) casseroles. These and the pottery ones are both OK. Don't get them really hot and then put them in cold water or they may crack.

There are a bewildering number of sizes, but get one that holds at least 2 litres or 4 pints.

Our personal recommendation must be for a cast-iron casserole. The ideal size is a 25 cm oval casserole with straight sides. It holds 4 litres (7 pints) and can take a chicken, a small leg of lamb or most beef roasts, as well as being OK for all the casserole dishes in the book. It is fairly foolproof. It also means there is lots of juice for making gravy.

Large ovenproof dish

These come in all sizes. They can be made from pottery, ovenproof glass or metal. If you get a big enough one it can be used as a roasting dish as well.

The most useful one we use is 30 cm by 18 cm (11$\frac{1}{2}$ by 7$\frac{1}{2}$

11

inches) and 6 cm (2 inches) deep and made of ovenproof glass. It is big enough to roast a chicken in, or make Lasagne or Shepherd's Pie.

Round ovenproof glass dish 25 cm (10 inches) diameter

This is used for cooking tarts and quiches, and doubles as something you can roast chicken pieces on.

Metal baking sheet about 25 cm (10 inches) across

This can be used for quickly warming things in the oven or cooking things that don't create a lot of liquid. It will also do as a tin to cook or heat pizzas and pizza bases.

Colander or sieve

This is useful for draining vegetables after they have been washed, and again after they have been cooked or for draining cooked pasta.

Colanders come in metal and plastic, with and without bases. The ones with bases will stand up on their own so you can put them in the sink and keep your hands away from the boiling substances you pour in. Plastic ones are cheaper.

Sieves can do most of what a colander does. They don't come with stands, but do have long handles. You can drain rice in them. You can also use a sieve as a fine strainer, to get the lumps out of gravy or sauce.

Grater

These are made from metal or plastic and have a range of cutting surfaces for getting different sizes of gratings. Use these for grating cheese, carrot or whatever.

Pie dish (if you want pies)

A metal dish, coated with non-stick material. It should be about 22 cm (8½ inches) across, with sloping sides at least 3 cm (1 inch) deep. Some have lots of holes in the bottom which help make the pastry base crisp. Other dishes are pottery. This dish is for making pies, which have a pastry lid as opposed to tarts which don't.

BITS THAT MAKE LIFE EASIER

Lemon zester

This is for getting the rind off lemons and oranges. It has four or five holes in a little scraper. There is no other tool which does it as quickly, or that makes such long strips of rind. If you use a knife and then slice it, the shreds come out a bit big. You can try using a grater, but it's not as easy.

Apple corer

A sharp-ended tube on a handle. You push the corer through the apple from the top of the apple where the stalk would be. When you pull it out it takes the core and seeds out.

Garlic crusher

There's not a lot to say about these. You put the peeled garlic in and squeeze the handles together. The garlic gets pulped up. You poke the residue out and throw it away.

Garlic is available ready pulped in tubes or jars.

Wok

A wok is like a combination of a frying-pan and saucepan. There are a number of Wok kits which include the Wok itself (a sort of metal bowl with a handle), lid, chopsticks, spoon and whatever else is thought to be useful. They are the best thing to cook Chinese stir-fry in.

Authentic woks do not have a non-stick coating, but others do. Get one with a non-stick coating, but remember not to use metal tools on it. Also, buy one with a flat bottom (round ones can be unstable).

Larger woks are particularly useful. You can use them to cook larger quantities of food like chilli con carne or curries.

GET A CUPBOARD

It is worth having some ingredients that you keep in store. There is no need to go and get them all at once but if you buy a few at a time you will have enough stuff to cook at least a meal. The idea is that you can cope with emergencies, like forgetting you have someone coming round, or coming in late, starving hungry.

There are some things which you don't use up every time you cook a recipe which includes it.

Cans and things

Salt and pepper, preferably a pepper grinder
400 g tin of plum tomatoes
500 g pack of pasta
Sunflower oil
Olive oil
Tikka powder
Packet of mixed Mediterranean herbs
Pack of Mexican chilli seasoning
400 g tin of red kidney beans
Tin of baked beans
200 g tin of tuna
Carton of custard

Fridge

Tube of garlic paste
Mayonnaise
Small bottle of lemon juice
Butter or low fat spread
Eggs
Tomato purée

Frozen food

1 pack of chicken pieces (thighs, breasts or quarters)
1 pack of white fish (Cod, Hake or Hoki)

Vegetables

Onions
Potatoes
Red pepper

There are the basics for pasta and tomato sauce, Mediterranean Fish or Italian Roast Chicken.

When you have used up any of the ingredients, replace it.

HOW TO . . .

HOW TO COOK VEGETABLES

Frozen

For frozen peas, sweet corn and other vegetables, follow the instructions on the bag. In general these will include adding the vegetables to boiling water with half a teaspoon of salt, and cooking for a few minutes. Cooking times are approximately 3 minutes for sweet corn (off the cob) and 5 minutes for peas.

Fresh

Fresh vegetables take a bit more preparation than frozen and sometimes take longer than frozen vegetables to cook. There are times in the year when fresh vegetables will be much cheaper than frozen, and other times when they will be more expensive or simply unavailable.

Wash all fresh vegetables thoroughly. Throw away any leaves which are slimy and cut out any bits that look bad.

Potatoes

Potatoes are probably the most widely used and versatile vegetable. They can be boiled, baked, roasted, mashed, deep fried as chips or pan fried in butter.

New potatoes have thin flaky skins which almost come off when the potatoes are scrubbed. They are smaller, often called 'Jersey Royals' or 'Cyprus'. They are good for boiling or salads.

Old potatoes are larger, go under such names as Whites, King Edwards, Désirée Reds or Romanos. Good for mashing, roasting or baking.

Boiled potatoes

Potatoes can be cooked with their skins on or off. They are better for you with the skins on. If you are leaving their skins on be sure to give them a thorough wash or scrub and dig out any eyes or unpleasant looking bits.

Cook small to medium potatoes whole. Large ones should be cut in half or quarters, so that all the pieces of potatoes in the saucepan are about the same size. Generally speaking the smaller the potato piece the quicker it will cook. Put the potatoes in a saucepan of water with 1 teaspoon of salt, bring to the boil, turn the heat down and simmer for 20–25 minutes. Test them with a fork to see if they are done. When they are done the fork will easily pierce the potato. If they start to fall apart they are overdone. When they are done drain off the water and serve.

Mashed potatoes

Peel and cook as for boiled potatoes (above), and then drain off the water. Put them in a bowl or return them to the saucepan, then mash the potatoes up with a fork or a potato masher. Add small blobs of butter or margarine and fresh ground pepper to taste. If you like them creamier add a little milk (1 tablespoon) and mix well into the mashed potatoes.

Baked potatoes

Pick large old potatoes for this. Get about three potatoes to the kilogram. Do not peel, but give them a good scrub. Stick a metal skewer through each potato, it helps them to cook in the middle. If you like the skin very crispy then prick the skin with a fork and place on the top shelf of the oven on 230°C, 450°F, Gas mark 8 for about an hour.

To check if they are done, cover your hand, preferably with an oven glove, to protect it from the heat and squeeze the sides gently. If it gives easily, it is done. If you like it less crispy, cover in tin foil and remove ten minutes before taking from the oven. If not crispy at all, leave the tin foil on.

Roast potatoes

Peel the potatoes, cutting away any nasty bits, and cutting out any eyes. Chop the potatoes in half if medium sized or into quarters if large. Put the potatoes in an ovenproof dish with some sunflower oil. Turn over the potatoes to coat them in oil. Cook in the top of a preheated oven at 180°C, 350°F, Gas mark 4 for 60 minutes or so if you like them really well done. Turn over half-way through cooking.

You can heat the oil first by putting the dish with the oil in the oven for about 10 minutes before adding the vegetables. It helps to reduce sticking.

Pan fried potato in butter

This is a good way of using up cooked, left-over potato. Just put a couple of spoons of butter in a frying-pan. Slice the potato and fry for about 10 minutes.

Chips

We are not going to cover chips in this book; there are so many kinds of oven chips and frozen chips available and so many chip shops that it is not worth the hassle and risk of cooking them. Chip pans are the most common cause of household fire in the country.

Carrots

This is a vegetable that is good eaten raw. Add grated carrot to salad, or cut them into large match-stick shapes to dip into things like guacamole.

They are good roasted, and can be peeled and cooked together in the same dish as a joint of meat.

To cook separately, just peel and chop into quarters lengthways and put in an ovenproof dish with half a cup of water, a tablespoon of butter and a teaspoon of sugar. Cover with foil and cook in a preheated oven at 180°C, 350°F, Gas mark 4 for 30 minutes.

Small, young carrots can be boiled whole for 10 minutes or steamed whole for 20 minutes.

Cauliflower or broccoli

Break into 'florets' then cook in 5 cm (2 inches) of water with a teaspoon of salt for about 10 minutes. Test the florets with a fork to check if they are ready. Cauliflower and broccoli can be eaten raw, and the longer you cook them, the softer they get.

Cabbage

This comes in several colours. red, white and green. Treat them all the same. Throw away any nasty looking outer leaves. Cut out the central hard core and discard. Chop the cabbage roughly and cook in 2 cm (1 inch) of water with a teaspoon of salt for about 10–20 minutes.

Red and white cabbage are good shredded raw in salads particularly in the winter when lettuces are very expensive or hard to find.

Spinach

This is good raw as a salad leaf or lightly cooked. It shrinks when cooked so you will need at least 500g (1 lb) of spinach for two people.

First wash the spinach, shake out the excess water. Put the spinach into a saucepan with salt to taste and a blob (the size of a small walnut) of butter. There is no need to add any more water. Cook the spinach in a medium-sized saucepan over a medium heat. As soon as the water on the leaves starts to hiss and bubble, and the butter to melt, stir the spinach gently. When it is floppy and transparent, two to three minutes later, it is cooked. Strain off the liquid and serve.

Broad beans, runner beans, fine beans, sugar snaps and mange tout

All these small beans and peas are eaten in the pod. Cut off both ends, and pull any stringy bits from down the side. Cut them into pieces, except the sugar snaps and mange tout which should be cooked whole. Just cover with water, add salt to taste and boil rapidly for five to ten minutes until tender, testing them with a fork. Sugar snaps and mange tout only take three minutes.

Corn on the cob

This is a cheap vegetable in the summer and almost a meal in itself. There are several ways to cook corn: it can be boiled, baked or barbecued.

If boiling, pull all the leaves off and boil in salted water for 20–30 minutes. Check with a fork to see if the corn is soft enough to eat. The fork should pierce the corn easily. Serve with a blob of butter and freshly ground black pepper.

If barbecuing, keep the leaves on, and barbecue for 10–20 minutes turning a couple of times. If the leaves have been removed by the shop, don't worry, just turn the corn more often.

If baking the corn, pull the leaves off as for boiling, place on a baking tray, put a little oil or butter on the corn, sprinkle with salt and pepper and bake for about 45 minutes.

Courgettes

Courgettes are quick and easy to cook. Wash them and slice either across or lengthways. Put them in a pan with some oil or butter and some seasoning. Cook on a medium heat for about five minutes and serve.

HOW TO COOK RICE

The most important thing to know about cooking rice is that you should use twice as much water as you do rice. Below is a recipe for plain boiled rice for two people.

Serves 2   ⏲ *Preparation 1 min, Cooking time depends on sort of rice – Easy*

INGREDIENTS
1 cup rice
2 cups water
1 teaspoon salt

EQUIPMENT
Saucepan with lid
Measuring cups and spoons

METHOD
Read the packet to get the correct cooking time. Put the rice, water and salt in the pan. Bring the water and rice to the boil, stirring once to stop the rice sticking to the bottom of the pan. Turn down the heat to low. Put the lid on the pan. Cook for the correct time until the fluid is absorbed (see below for different timings). Do not stir!

After the cooking time, take it off the heat and let it stand for a couple of minutes. Fluff it up with a fork to separate the grains and serve.

TIPS
The cup referred to is a standard measuring cup of 250 ml. It is approximately the same as a mug. For larger quantities just use 1 cup of water and half a cup of rice per person.

Basmati is more fragrant than long grain, and also more forgiving, because it holds together during cooking.

Approximate cooking times (read the packet for more accurate timings):

Basmati	10 minutes
American long grain	15 minutes
Organic long grain brown rice	30–35 minutes
Brown quick cook	20–25 minutes

HOW TO COOK NOODLES

Serves 2   ⏲ *Preparation 1 min, Cooking 4 min – Easy*

INGREDIENTS
2 sheets dried noodles
1 tablespoon sesame oil

EQUIPMENT
Saucepan
Sieve or colander to drain the noodles

METHOD
Check the cooking time on the packet. Boil at least a pint of water in a saucepan. Put the noodles in the water. Boil for about 4 minutes. Drain the noodles. Return to the pan. Add a tablespoon of sesame oil and stir round. Serve.

TIPS
You get three sheets of noodles in a 250 g pack of Sharwoods medium noodles.

HOW TO COOK PASTA

Serves 2 ⏱ *Preparation 1 min, Cooking 2–10 min – Easy*

INGREDIENTS
250 g dried pasta (generally half a pack or two and a half cups)
1 teaspoon salt

EQUIPMENT
Saucepan
Wooden spoon
Sieve or colander

METHOD
Read the packet for the correct cooking time. Put at least a pint of water into the saucepan and bring to the boil. Put the pasta in the water. Stir the pasta once to stop it sticking to the bottom of the pan. Bring back to the boil and simmer for as long as the packet says. Add the salt.

The best way to judge if the pasta is cooked is to bite it. This is tricky, because if you fish out a bit and stick it in your mouth you may burn your mouth with the boiling water. Wait a bit and blow on it, then bite it.

You can trust the cooking time if you want to or put a bit on a plate and cut it with the edge of a fork. If it is hard it needs longer. If it is like mush it is overcooked.

HOW TO ROLL PASTRY

INGREDIENTS
Half a 500 g pack of pastry, chilled or frozen
2 tablespoons flour

EQUIPMENT
Rolling pin

METHOD
Make sure the pastry is well thawed, four hours in the fridge being typical. Keep the pastry in the fridge before rolling. Make sure that the surface that you are going to roll on is clean, dry and flat. Pastry can stick to the surface or rolling pin unless it is kept dry, so sprinkle the surface and the pastry with flour.

Roll and then turn the pastry through a quarter of a circle. Roll and turn, scattering more flour if needed.

It is remarkably easy.

HOW TO BAKE A PASTRY CASE

METHOD
A few recipes need a pre-cooked pastry case to work. If you put the filling in the raw pastry case it will not cook properly. If you just cook the case in the oven it will distort and shrink. So part cook it without the proper filling but lined with greaseproof paper and with some dried beans to keep the pastry in place.

Roll out the pastry, as shown above. Line the dish. Pastry is fairly flexible so you can push it into place. If it tears patch it with a spare bit, moistening with a bit of water to make sure it sticks. Pastry shrinks when it cooks so if you trim it to the top of the rim it will shrink below that level. So cut it high.

Prick the bottom of the pastry with a fork at least five times to let steam out. Cut a piece of greaseproof paper and press gently on to the pastry. Fill the bottom with a layer of cheap dried beans, for instance butter beans. Cook the pastry case at 200°C, 400°F, Gas mark 6 for 15 minutes until the top edges go golden.

Take the pastry case out of the oven.

HOW TO MAKE DRIED BEANS TURN OUT SOFT AND NOT LIKE BULLETS

① Preparation 5 min, Cooking time depends – Easy

INGREDIENTS
1½ cups of dried beans or chick peas – equivalent to 2 (440 g) tins

EQUIPMENT
Saucepan with lid
Bowl

METHOD
Check over the dried beans. Throw away any stones or odd looking ones. Put the beans in a plastic bowl or one made from heatproof glass. Pour boiling water on top of them, and cover to a depth of about 5 cm (2 inches). (Don't add any salt until the beans are cooked.) This takes about a litre or two pints. Leave the beans for 1 to 2 hours to swell up, preferably in a fridge. Drain and rinse the beans.

Put them in a saucepan with at least a pint of fresh water. Bring to the boil and boil vigorously for 10 minutes. Turn down the heat until the water is just simmering gently. Cook the beans till they are soft. This may take anything between 30 minutes and two and a half hours depending on the variety. Add more water if it gets low.

When the beans are done, take off the heat. Drain the beans and leave to cool down.

ADDITIONS & ALTERNATIVES

Approximate cooking times (read the packet for more accurate timings):

Red kidney beans	60–90 minutes
Chick peas	150 minutes
Rose coco (Borlotti) beans	150 minutes
Red split lentils	30 minutes
Green lentils with skin on	90 minutes

TIPS

Parsley is reputed to reduce the wind generating capacity of beans.

HOW TO DEFROST THINGS

Chicken pieces

Overnight in the fridge or six hours at room temperature.

Chicken livers (200 g or 8 oz tub)

Four hours at room temperature or overnight in the fridge.

Lamb chops

Defrost in a single layer for four hours at room temperature or overnight in the fridge.

Half leg of lamb

Overnight in the fridge or four hours at room temperature.

Whole chicken (1.5 kg or 3 lb)

24 hours in fridge, 12 hours in a cool room.

Packet of extra large prawns

Three hours at room temperature.

Plaice, cod and haddock

Cook from frozen.

CHILLI

FRESH CHILLI – A WARNING! When you chop up the chillies be careful to avoid getting juice on your hands. It will sting. If you touch your eyes, mouth or other sensitive areas even an hour after chopping them they will smart and burn. So wash your hands or wear rubber gloves.

STARTERS

TUNA MAYONNAISE

Makes a small bowl   ① *Preparation 5 min – Easy*

INGREDIENTS
200 g tin of tuna
2 or 3 spring onions
2 tablespoons mayonnaise
Salt and pepper to taste

EQUIPMENT
Tin opener
Small bowl
Sharp knife
Chopping board
Fork
Set of measuring spoons

METHOD
Open the tin of tuna. Drain the liquid from the tin. Put the tuna in the bowl and mash it up with the fork.

Get the spring onions and take off the outer leaves. Cut off the root end and trim off the green leaves and any other unsavoury bits. Wash the spring onions and dry. Chop the onions into thin rings with the knife.

Mix the onions and the mayonnaise in with the tuna. Add salt and pepper, if you wish.

ADDITIONS & ALTERNATIVES

This can be used as a pasta sauce. Mix the tuna mayonnaise in with freshly cooked and drained pasta shapes or spaghetti. Sprinkle with grated Parmesan cheese and fresh ground pepper, and serve with fresh warm bread and salad.

Use it as a filling for baked potato.

Use in an avocado pear as below.

AVOCADO VINAIGRETTE, PRAWN OR TUNA

2 servings   ① *Preparation 10 min – Easy*

INGREDIENTS

1 ripe avocado
3 tablespoons olive oil
1 tablespoon lemon juice or wine vinegar
Salt and pepper

EQUIPMENT

Sharp knife
Chopping board
Set of measuring spoons
Small jam jar with lid

METHOD

Cut the avocado in half. Discard the stone.

Put the oil, lemon juice, salt and pepper in a jam jar and shake vigorously. It will go thick and creamy. Pour into the hole left by the avocado stone.

ADDITIONS & ALTERNATIVES

Serve with brown bread and butter.

You can buy many different ready-made vinaigrette sauces.

Try making different flavour vinaigrettes using walnut or sunflower oil instead of olive oil, or orange juice instead of the lemon, or adding a crushed clove of garlic, half a teaspoon of French mustard or herbs.

Use Tuna mayonnaise instead of the vinaigrette.

Put a few thawed prawns in the hole and serve with vinaigrette. You can use prawns and prawn cocktail sauce, which fortunately is the next recipe.

TIPS

Ripe avocados are still green and are not hard, but should 'give' a bit when gently pressed.

Make this just before you want to eat. If you cut the avocado too soon it will discolour.

PRAWN COCKTAIL

2 big or 4 small servings   ① *Preparation 10 min – Easy*

INGREDIENTS

Iceberg lettuce
250 g pack of frozen or fresh cooked prawns
2 tablespoons mayonnaise
2 tablespoons low fat yoghurt (or 2 more tablespoons
    of mayonnaise)
1 or 2 teaspoons tomato ketchup
1 or 2 teaspoons lemon juice
$\frac{1}{2}$ teaspoon paprika
1 lemon, sliced

EQUIPMENT
Small mixing bowl
Set of measuring spoons
Sharp knife
Chopping board
2 small cereal or soup bowls or 4 wineglasses

METHOD
Wash and dry a few leaves of iceberg lettuce. Put the lettuce in the bottom of a wineglass or small bowl. Divide up the prawns and put them on the lettuce, keeping a few aside to dangle over the side of the bowl.

Mix the mayonnaise, yoghurt, ketchup, lemon juice and paprika in the bowl. Pour some on each portion. Finish off with a couple of good-looking prawns and a slice of lemon.

ADDITIONS & ALTERNATIVES
Serve with toast or brown bread.

Use white crab meat or lobster bits chopped up instead of prawns.

If you like a more spicy sauce add two drops of Tabasco sauce or a pinch of cayenne pepper to it.

This is a very flexible sauce and can be used with avocado and prawn. It also makes a good dip for Kettle chips.

Add a small pot of cottage cheese and some prawns, and eat it with salads. This is also good with crisps or tortilla chips.

MELON & PARMA HAM

Serves 4 ⏱ *Preparation 5 min – Easy*

INGREDIENTS
1 ripe Galia or Honeydew melon
8 thin slices Parma or Serano ham

EQUIPMENT
Sharp knife
Chopping board

METHOD
Cut the melon into quarters. Scrape away the seeds with a spoon and discard. Cut the melon away from the skin and chop into neat large cubes.

Arrange the melon and the ham on four plates.

ADDITIONS & ALTERNATIVES
Parma and Serano ham should be cut very thin so they are translucent. They are available in packets or from the delicatessen counter or specialist shops. Serano is slightly moister and pinker. It should not be hard.

If the counter does not sell much it can be like an old boot. Don't let them give you the dried out top slices.

Try other melons.

TIPS
Ripe melons smell sweet and are slightly softer, particularly at the end where the stalk comes out.

You can get a small scoop which makes melon balls.

SMOKED MACKEREL PATÉ

Serves 2 or 4   ⏲ *Preparation 10 min – Easy*

INGREDIENTS
2 smoked mackerel fillets with peppercorns
2 to 3 tablespoons butter or soft margarine
1 teaspoon lemon juice
Toast or crusty bread

EQUIPMENT
Fork
Bowl
Set of measuring spoons

METHOD
Pull the skin off the mackerel fillets. Break the fish into lumps, put in bowl and mash up with the butter and lemon juice until smooth enough to spread.

If not spreadable, mash more or add a bit more butter.

Serve with toast or fresh crusty bread.

SMOKED SALMON SALAD

Serves 2   ⏲ *Preparation 15 min, Cooking 12 min – Easy*

INGREDIENTS
1 egg
4 lettuce leaves
100 g packet smoked salmon
100 g pot lumpfish roe, red or black
1 lemon
Bread and butter or toast
Freshly ground pepper to taste

EQUIPMENT
Saucepan
Sharp knife
Chopping board

METHOD
To hard boil the egg, put it in a small saucepan nearly full of water. Bring to the boil, and boil for ten minutes. Cool the egg by putting it in cold water.

When the egg is cold, take off the shell. Chop the egg up. It is easier to chop the white separately then lightly mash the yolk.

Wash the lettuce leaves. Shake dry. Arrange the clean lettuce leaves on two plates. Arrange the salmon artistically in a manner befitting the plate and the occasion. Put half the egg on each plate and a teaspoon of lumpfish roe on top. Cut the lemon in quarters and put one or two on each plate.

Serve with bread and butter or toast and freshly ground pepper.

ADDITIONS & ALTERNATIVES
Assemble the ingredients into a sandwich.

Use smoked salmon trout. It tastes just as good and is cheaper.

TIPS
The egg may be prepared earlier. Leave it in its shell till ready to make the rest of the salad.

STUFFED TOMATOES WITH PESTO

Serves 4   ① *Preparation 3 min – Easy*

INGREDIENTS
4 large tomatoes
190 g jar basil pesto
Salt and freshly ground pepper to taste
2 tablespoons olive oil
Bread and butter
Green salad

EQUIPMENT
Sharp knife
Chopping board
Set of measuring spoons

METHOD
Cut the tomatoes in half. Scoop out the seeds. Put a teaspoon of pesto in each half. Season with salt and pepper. Dribble a little olive oil on each one.

Serve with bread and a little green salad.

STUFFED TOMATOES WITH SPICED FILLING

Serves 4   ⏱ *Preparation 5 min, Cooking 10 min – Easy*

INGREDIENTS
1 egg
1 tablespoon hot mango chutney
2 tablespoons mayonnaise
Salt and freshly ground pepper to taste
4 medium to large tomatoes
Bread and butter
Green salad

EQUIPMENT
Saucepan
Bowl
Sharp knife
Fork
Chopping board
Set of measuring spoons

METHOD
To hard boil the egg, boil it in the saucepan for ten minutes, then cool it down by running cold water over it for five minutes.

Put the hot mango chutney in the bowl. Chop up any lumps.

Peel the egg and mash up with the chutney. Add the mayonnaise. Mix together and season.

Cut the tomatoes in half. Scoop out the seeds. Put a teaspoon of the filling in each half.

Serve with bread and a little green salad.

GRILLED GRAPEFRUIT

Serves 2   ℗ *Preparation 2 min, Cooking 5 to 10 min – Easy*

INGREDIENTS
1 grapefruit
1 tablespoon port or brandy (optional)
2 tablespoons brown sugar

EQUIPMENT
Sharp knife
Chopping board
Grill
Set of measuring spoons

METHOD
Cut the grapefruit in half. Dig out any visible pips. Loosen the segments by cutting between them. Put half the port or brandy on each half. Sprinkle the sugar over the top. Cook under a moderate grill for five to ten minutes.

ROCKET & GOAT'S CHEESE SALAD

Serves 4 as a starter   ℗ *Preparation 10 min – Easy*

Good as a starter for four or as a summer meal with other salad.

INGREDIENTS
1 packet of Rocket about 100g
175 g (6 oz) of mild goat's cheese
1 clove of garlic
3 tablespoons olive oil
1 tablespoon lemon juice

Salt and pepper
1 teaspoon of ground almonds (optional)

EQUIPMENT

Sharp knife
Chopping board
Garlic crusher
Jam jar with lid
Set of measuring spoons

METHOD

Look at the leaves and throw away any slimy ones. Wash the rest in water and then drain and pat dry between kitchen towel. Lay them out on a plate. Cut the goat's cheese into chunks. Distribute them on the Rocket leaves.

Peel and crush the garlic into the jam jar. Put all of the other dressing ingredients in the jam jar and shake for 30 seconds. Pour over the salad.

ADDITIONS & ALTERNATIVES

Use Camembert or Brie instead of the goat's cheese.

Use salad and basil leaves or watercress instead of the Rocket.

Add two shredded sun-dried tomatoes to the dressing.

There's a cooked version where the cheese is left to stand for half an hour in the dressing then dipped in breadcrumbs and put in the oven at 180°C, 350°F, Gas mark 4 for three minutes.

TIPS

Prepared garlic is sold in tubes and jars. Just read the tube or jar for the suggested equivalent amount. It keeps for six weeks in the fridge.

Rocket is a spicy, peppery green herb. It tastes similar to watercress. Larger supermarkets have it for sale already prepared.

SMOKED SALMON ROLL

Serves 4   ① *Preparation 10 min, Cooking 5 min – Moderate*

INGREDIENTS

2 eggs
1 tablespoon milk
Salt and freshly ground pepper to taste
1 tablespoon butter for frying
100 g (4 oz) packet of smoked salmon or smoked salmon trout
Green salad leaves (lettuce)

EQUIPMENT

Bowl
Set of measuring spoons
Fork
20 cm (8 inch) frying-pan
Egg/fish slice (to turn the omelette over)
Chopping board
Sharp knife

METHOD

First make an omelette. Break eggs into bowl and add milk. Add a pinch of salt and pinch of pepper. Beat with a fork until mixed.

Melt the butter in the frying-pan over a medium heat. Add the egg mixture. After 30 seconds it will be solid underneath and can be turned over for another minute or so. Put the omelette on the chopping board. Let it cool down a bit.

Put the salmon slices on the omelette. Roll up the omelette so you have a kind of Swiss roll effect. Cut the roll into slices and arrange on plates with the salad leaves.

ADDITIONS & ALTERNATIVES

Put a tinned anchovy on each roll.

GARLIC MUSHROOMS

Serves 4   ⏲ *Preparation 3 min plus an hour in the fridge,*
Cooking 5 min – Easy

INGREDIENTS
2 tablespoons chopped parsley
350 g (13 oz) mushrooms
3 cloves garlic
2 tablespoons wine vinegar
2 tablespoons olive oil
Salt and pepper
2 tablespoons tomato purée

EQUIPMENT
Sharp knife
Chopping board
Saucepan
Set of measuring spoons
Bowl

METHOD
Wash, drain, dry and finely chop the parsley. Wipe the mushrooms clean. Discard any nasty ones. Chop the end off the stalks.

Peel and chop the garlic. Put the garlic, vinegar, oil, salt and pepper in the pan together with about half a cup of water. Boil the mixture. Add the mushrooms and the tomato purée. Boil for five minutes, stirring.

Take the pan off the heat. Allow to cool and put in a bowl with the parsley in the fridge. Leave to get really cold.

ADDITIONS & ALTERNATIVES
Try lemon juice instead of vinegar.

Add 1 teaspoon of Mediterranean mixed herbs.

TIPS

Prepared garlic is sold in tubes and jars. Just read the tube or jar for the suggested equivalent amount. It keeps for six weeks in the fridge.

Tomato purée comes in tubes. It keeps for four weeks in the fridge.

CHICKEN LIVER PATÉ

Serves 2 to 4   ① *Preparation 5 min, Cooking 12 min – Easy*

INGREDIENTS
225 g (9 oz) tub frozen chicken livers
2 small to medium onions
2 cloves of garlic
1 tablespoon butter for cooking
$\frac{1}{2}$ teaspoon mixed herbs
Salt and freshly ground pepper to taste
Toast

EQUIPMENT
Sharp knife
Chopping board
Frying-pan
Wooden spoon
Set of measuring spoons
Bowl

METHOD
Defrost chicken livers. This takes four hours at room temperature or overnight in the fridge.

Chop the onions and garlic. Melt the butter in the frying-pan on a low flame. Add the onions and garlic and gently cook till they are soft. Add the chicken livers and herbs. Cook together gently for ten minutes, mashing it a bit with the spoon to check it is cooked through. If you cook too high it will turn out like rubber.

Put it all in the bowl and mash it together until it is spreadable and to your taste. Some like it chunkier than others. Season to taste.

Serve cold with toast.

ADDITIONS & ALTERNATIVES
Add 1 tablespoon of sherry to the frying-pan when it is nearly cooked through.

TIPS
This will keep in the fridge for a day.

Prepared garlic is sold in tubes and jars. Just read the tube or jar for the suggested equivalent amount. It keeps for six weeks in the fridge.

FRIED CAMEMBERT & CRANBERRY SAUCE

Serves 2–4   ① *Preparation 5 min, Cooking 3 min – Moderate*

INGREDIENTS
A small Camembert cheese (not ripe and runny, and keep it in the
     fridge before use)
1 tablespoon flour
1 beaten egg
2 tablespoons breadcrumbs
Oil
Green salad
300 g (11 oz) jar of cranberry sauce

EQUIPMENT
Knife
Set of measuring spoons
3 small bowls
Frying-pan

METHOD
Cut the cheese into eight segments. Roll the cheese in the flour, dip into the beaten egg and then coat in breadcrumbs.

Heat the oil in the frying-pan. Fry the cheese for about three minutes till golden brown.

Serve immediately with a green salad and cranberry sauce.

ADDITIONS & ALTERNATIVES
You can grate or food-process your own breadcrumbs.

Use Brie instead of Camembert

Use gooseberry preserve instead of cranberry sauce.

HOT WHISKY SMOKED FISH

Serves 4 or eat two yourself for a main course

*℗ Preparation 15 min,
Cooking 40 min – Moderately fiddly and messy but worth it*

INGREDIENTS
500 g (1 lb) smoked haddock
1 cup milk for cooking the haddock in
1 medium carton (284 ml or 10 fl oz) of single cream
2 tablespoons whisky
400 g tin plum tomatoes
4 tablespoons grated Parmesan cheese
Salt and freshly ground pepper to taste

EQUIPMENT
Sharp knife
Chopping board
Saucepan
Small bowl
Fork
4 ovenproof ramekins or an ovenproof dish
Set of measuring spoons
Tin opener

METHOD
Peel the skin off the haddock. Put the milk and the haddock in the saucepan and bring to the boil. The fish will go firm within a couple of minutes. Take the fish off the heat. Drain off the milk and put the fish into the bowl. Let it cool down. Flake it apart and divide it into the four ramekins

Put the single cream and the whisky in the bowl and mix together.

Open the tin of tomatoes and drain off the juice. Lift out the tomatoes. Cut each one in half and discard the seeds. Put a piece of tomato on top of each portion of fish. Pour the cream and whisky into the ramekins. Put about one tablespoon of Parmesan cheese on top of each ramekin and season. Cook in a preheated oven at 200°C, 400°F, Gas mark 6.

ADDITIONS & ALTERNATIVES
Use grated Pecorino cheese. Both it and Parmesan can be bought in packets.

TIPS
Prepare this a while before you want to eat it. Letting the fish stand in the whisky makes the flavour even better.

A ramekin is a small circular pot roughly 5 cm (2 inches) tall, and 8 cm (3 inches) across. They are also good for making individual desserts in like chocolate mousse or cream caramel.

SNACKS

PRAWN DIP

Enough for large pack of crisps
or tortilla chips   ⓘ *Preparation 2 min – Easy*

INGREDIENTS
Half a 250 g pack of frozen prawns
1 medium carton (about 227 g or 8 oz) cottage cheese
1 tablespoon tomato ketchup
1 teaspoon paprika
1 tablespoon lemon juice

EQUIPMENT
Bowl
Set of measuring spoons

METHOD
Thaw the prawns for at least two hours, or according to the pack.
If you are in a hurry, put them in a sieve and run them under
COLD water, then squeeze dry. Mix in the rest of the ingredients.

ADDITIONS & ALTERNATIVES
Serve with crisps, Kettle chips, tortilla chips, or chopped veget-
ables.
   Can be a meal with salad.

TAHINI CREAM DIP

Makes a small bowl   ⏲ *Preparation 2 min – Easy*

INGREDIENTS
1 small carton (142 ml or 5 fl oz) of unsweetened
    Greek yoghurt
1 tablespoon Tahini

EQUIPMENT
Bowl
Fork
Set of measuring spoons

METHOD
Mix the Tahini and the yoghurt together. It will make the yoghurt
thicker.

ADDITIONS & ALTERNATIVES
Tahini Cream is a sauce for falafel (spicy fried chick pea balls).
Serve with salad and hot pitta bread.
    It also makes a good salad dressing.
    Adjust the ratio of Tahini to yoghurt.
    Try adding lemon juice and sesame oil to thin it a bit.
    Add fresh chopped herbs, particularly coriander, parsley, mint
or chives.

TIPS
Tahini is a paste made up of crushed sesame seeds. It is available
from health food shops and larger supermarkets.

HUMMUS & PITTA BREAD

Serves 4   ① *Preparation 5 min – Easy*

INGREDIENTS
250 g pot hummus
1 tablespoon Tahini
1 tablespoon olive oil
Pitta bread

EQUIPMENT
Plate
Set of measuring spoons
Spoon
Grill
Sharp knife
Chopping board

METHOD
Spoon the hummus on to a plate. Use the back of a spoon to level the hummus. Make a slight depression in the middle of the plate and fill it with the Tahini. Make another slight indentation round the plate near the edge. Fill this with the olive oil.

Grill the pitta bread and cut into slices.

Serve.

ADDITIONS & ALTERNATIVES
Put a couple of olives and a teaspoon of chopped parsley on top.

Eat with tortilla chips.

BASIC CHEESE ON TOAST

Serves 1   ⏱ *Preparation 2 min, Cooking 3 min – Easy*

INGREDIENTS
1 slice toast
Cheddar cheese (about 50 g or 2 oz)
Enough butter for a slice of toast

EQUIPMENT
Sharp knife
Chopping board
Grill

METHOD
Butter the toast. Slice the cheese and put it on the toast. Grill the cheese until it is runny and brown.

SMART CHEESE ON TOAST

Serves 1   ⏱ *Preparation 3 min, Cooking 3 min – Easy*

INGREDIENTS
1 slice toast
Enough butter for a slice of toast
Cheddar cheese (about 50 g or 2 oz or a cup of grated cheese)
1 tablespoon milk
1 teaspoon paprika

EQUIPMENT
Sharp knife
Cheese grater
Bowl

Set of measuring spoons
Grill pan

METHOD
Butter the toast. Grate the cheese. Mix it with the milk and paprika in the bowl. Spread the mixture on the toast. Grill the cheese until it is runny and brown.

ADDITIONS & ALTERNATIVES
Use ready grated cheese.

LATE CHEESE ON TOAST

Serves 1 ① *Preparation 3 min, Cooking 3 min – Easy*

INGREDIENTS
1 slice bread
Enough butter for the bread
1 small to medium onion
Cheddar cheese (about 50–75 g or 2–3 oz)
1 tablespoon HP Sauce

EQUIPMENT
Sharp knife
Chopping board
Set of measuring spoons
Grill

METHOD
Toast one side of the bread. Take it from under the grill. Butter the untoasted side.

Peel and chop the onion finely and sprinkle on the bread. Grill for a minute or so. Slice the cheese and put it on the toast. Grill the cheese until it is runny and brown. Pour HP sauce on the top.

ADDITIONS & ALTERNATIVES
Use ready grated cheese.
  Use cheese spread.

LATE TOASTED CHEESE SANDWICH

Serves 1   ⏱ *Preparation 3 min, Cooking 3 min – Easy*

INGREDIENTS
2 slices bread
2 tablespoons butter
HP Sauce
$\frac{1}{4}$ to $\frac{1}{2}$ onion
Cheddar cheese (about 50–75 g or 2–3 oz)
2 slices tomato

EQUIPMENT
Sharp knife
Chopping board
Grill
Set of measuring spoons

METHOD
Toast one slice of bread. Butter it. Toast one side of the other slice of bread. Take it from under the grill. Butter the untoasted side.
  Spread with HP Sauce.
  Peel and chop the onion finely and sprinkle on the bread. Grill for a minute or so. Slice the cheese and put it on the toast. Grill the cheese until it is runny and brown. Put the tomato and second slice of toast on top.

ADDITIONS & ALTERNATIVES
Use ready grated cheese.
  Add chopped ham.

FRIED CHEESE & ONION SANDWICH

Serves 1   ⏱ *Preparation 2 min, Cooking 5 min – Easy*

INGREDIENTS
2 slices bread
Enough butter for the bread
Sliced cheese (about 50 g or 2 oz)
2 slices of onion
1 tablespoon oil

EQUIPMENT
Sharp knife
Chopping board
Frying-pan
Set of measuring spoons

METHOD
Butter the bread. Make a cheese and onion sandwich.

Put the oil in the frying-pan. Heat. Fry the sandwich, turning once, till the cheese starts to melt.

Serve hot with a green salad, or on its own.

BACON & AVOCADO TOASTED SANDWICH

Serves 2   ⏱ *Preparation 5 min, Cooking 10 min – Easy*

INGREDIENTS
1 ripe avocado (ripe ones are not hard, but give a little at the end
    when gently pressed)
8 rashers bacon

4 slices bread
Freshly ground pepper
1 tablespoon mayonnaise

EQUIPMENT
Sharp knife
Chopping board
Grill
Set of measuring spoons

METHOD
Cut the avocado in half. Take out the stone.

Peel the avocado. Cut the avocado into slices. If it is really hard or horribly brown, throw it away and eat something else, like bacon and lettuce and tomato sandwich.

Cut nicks in the bacon rind every couple of centimetres (inch). This stops the bacon curling up. Grill for about five minutes a side, till cooked. Meanwhile, grill the bread. Put the bacon on two slices of toast. Put the avocado slices on the bacon. Grind some pepper on top. Spread a little mayonnaise on the other two slices of toast. Put these on top. Eat.

ADDITIONS & ALTERNATIVES
Bacon bought by the slice from the butcher is generally tastier than pre-packed bacon. There is quite a lot of extra water in pre-packed bacon, which gets added to make it sizzle, and a lot of salts.

You can fry bacon, but it does come out more oily.

If you like bacon less salty, cook it for two minutes, then run it under water. Return and continue cooking.

CLUB SANDWICH

Serves 2   ⏱ *Preparation 5 min, Cooking 10 min – Easy*

INGREDIENTS
A few lettuce leaves
1 ripe tomato
1 cup cooked chicken
4 to 6 rashers bacon
6 slices bread
2 tablespoons mayonnaise
2 tablespoons cranberry sauce
Pepper
A pack of Kettle chips

EQUIPMENT
Sharp knife
Chopping board
Grill
Set of measuring spoons
Set of measuring cups

METHOD
Wash and drain the lettuce. Wash and slice the tomato. Break up the chicken. Cut nicks in the bacon rind every couple of centimetres (inch). This stops the bacon curling up. If you prefer, just cut the rind off. Grill for about five minutes a side, till cooked.

Meanwhile, toast the bread. Spread a little mayonnaise on a slice of toast. Put on half the chicken and lettuce.

Spread some cranberry sauce on another bit of toast. Put this, cranberry side down, on the chicken. Put half the bacon on the top and then some sliced tomato. Grind some pepper on top. Spread a third bit of toast with some mayonnaise and place on top.

Repeat the assembly process for the second sandwich.

Serve with Kettle chips.

ADDITIONS & ALTERNATIVES

You can use turkey instead of chicken.

Bacon with rind is better than without. Bacon bought by the slice from the butcher is generally tastier than pre-packed bacon. There is quite a lot of extra water in pre-packed bacon, which gets added to make it sizzle, and a lot of salts. You can fry bacon, but it does come out more oily. If you like bacon less salty, cook it for 2 minutes, then run it under water. Return and continue cooking.

CHEAT'S CHOCOLATE CROISSANTS

Serves 2   ⏲ *Preparation 5 min, Cooking 20 min – Easy*

INGREDIENTS
375 g pack of ready rolled puff pastry
1 tablespoon butter
2 large chocolate flakes
1 teaspoon milk

EQUIPMENT
Sharp knife
Chopping board
Set of measuring spoons
Baking sheet

METHOD
Thaw the pastry according to the instructions on the packet. Four hours in the fridge seems typical. Unfold and cut into four pieces. Spread the pieces with a thin layer of butter.

Cut the flakes in half. Put one piece of flake on one piece of pastry. Roll it up. Seal the edge with a little milk. Do the other three. Put on a baking sheet and cook in a preheated oven at

200°C, 400°F, Gas mark 6 for about 15 to 20 minutes, until puffed up and golden brown.

ADDITIONS & ALTERNATIVES
Use chocolate bars or chocolate nut spread instead of flakes.

MINI GOURMET PIZZA

*Serves 4 as starter or summer
lunch with salad*

① *Preparation 5 min,
Cooking 10 min – Easy*

INGREDIENTS
1 ciabatta loaf
1 jar or tube sun-dried tomato paste
56 g (2 oz) tube of anchovy paste
Small (100 g) Mozzarella cheese
2 tablespoons olive oil
Salt and freshly ground pepper to taste
Salad of exotic leaves

EQUIPMENT
Sharp knife
Chopping board
Set of measuring spoons
Baking tray

METHOD
Cut 8 slices of ciabatta bread. Spread about a teaspoon of the sun-dried tomato sauce on each one. Spread an inch squirt of anchovy paste on each slice. Top off with a slice of Mozzarella cheese. Season with salt and pepper.

Wipe the baking tray with a little oil. Put the slices on the baking tray. Cook in a preheated oven at 200°C, 400°F, Gas mark

6 until the cheese is melted and slightly brown, about ten minutes.
Serve with a salad of some exotic leaves.

MINI PIZZA

Makes 6   ① *Preparation 5 min, Cooking 10 min – Easy*

INGREDIENTS
1 French loaf
200 g tube tomato purée
1 teaspoon oregano or mixed Mediterranean herbs
100 g Mozzarella cheese
50 g tin anchovies
1–2 tablespoons olive oil

EQUIPMENT
Sharp knife
Chopping board
Set of measuring spoons
Baking tray

METHOD
Cut the French loaf in half lengthways. Cut each slice into three.
Spread each piece with tomato purée. Sprinkle the herbs on the
tomato purée.

Cut the Mozzarella cheese into twelve slices. Arrange the
Mozzarella two slices to each 'pizza'. Put the anchovies on the top.
Brush the top with the oil. Cook in a preheated oven at 200°C,
400°F, Gas mark 6 until the Mozzarella is melted and slightly
brown, about 10 minutes.

ADDITIONS & ALTERNATIVES
Grill it.

Olives, sweet pepper rings or onion slices, all make good
toppings.

AUBERGINE WITH CHEESE

Makes a plateful   ① *Preparation 20 min, Cooking 15 min – Easy*

INGREDIENTS
2 medium aubergines
Olive oil
Cheese: Parmesan, Gouda, Monterey Jack or Cheddar

EQUIPMENT
Sharp knife
Chopping board
Frying-pan
Slotted spoon
Kitchen roll
Grill

METHOD
Slice the aubergines. Soak in water for 20 minutes, then drain and dry with kitchen paper.

Heat the oil in the frying-pan. Put some aubergine slices, so they do not overlap, in the hot oil. Cook and turn till they are golden on both sides, about three to five minutes. Lift out the aubergine slices and drain on a plate covered in kitchen roll. Cook the rest of the slices the same way.

Slice the cheese thinly and put one slice on each piece of aubergine. Put these on a grill pan and grill till the cheese is melting and brown.

These can be eaten hot, or cold as a summer meal with other Tapas and salad.

ADDITIONS & ALTERNATIVES
Dutch aubergines do not need soaking.

GRILLED SARDINES

Serves 4   ⏱ *Preparation 3 min, Cooking 20 min – Easy*

INGREDIENTS
10 fresh large sardines
1 tablespoon oil
1 lemon
Salt and pepper

EQUIPMENT
Knife
Grill
Set of measuring spoons

METHOD
Buy fresh sardines. Wash the fish under flowing water. Allow to dry. Put the sardines on a grill pan. Brush the sardines with a little oil. Cook for about ten minutes each side. Serve with lemon quarters, salt and pepper.

ADDITIONS & ALTERNATIVES
It goes well with salad.

TIPS
If you don't like fish heads, cut them off before cooking or buy them headless.

SALADS & DRESSINGS

Salads are quick and easy, and are some of the simplest things to experiment with. Salads may be just a few lettuce leaves but can be more complicated classic salads like Salad Niçoise, Waldorf Salad or Caesar Salad. This chapter has recipes for salad dressings and some brilliant salads.

Here is a bit of information on some salad ingredients, followed by some more unusual things you can use in salad. After that there are recipes for some classic and not so classic combinations.

Lettuces

The simplest salad is lettuce. There are a lot of different lettuces. Each has its own characteristics but they all make a good base for a green salad. Green salads are a lot less hassle than vegetables.

Go to your local street market or supermarket. Look at different lettuces, smell them and try them.

Iceberg lettuce is crisp and has a neutral taste. It can be sliced or cut into chunks. It keeps well in the fridge.

Webb's wonder is a crispish round lettuce.

Cos lettuce has long, crisp leaves good for dipping in things.

Round lettuce has more floppy leaves.

Oak leaf has crisp bitterish, brown and green leaves.

Radicchio is small and slightly bitterish, the colour of red cabbage with white veins.

Frisee and lollo rosso have wobbly edges to the leaves. The lollo rosso has purple or red edges to the leaves. Both are very decorative 'designer' lettuce.

Mixing together lettuces of different colour and textures works well.

If lettuce is not available, try shredding white or red cabbage.

Herbs

Fresh herbs can be used in salads, either as decoration or to give a more interesting flavour.

Basil is an aromatic herb, often used in Italian food.

Rocket has small leaves with a distinct taste like watercress.

Other herbs like parsley and coriander work well in salads.

Tomatoes

Ordinary tomatoes can be a bit tasteless but are available all year.

Cherry tomatoes are small, sweet and expensive.

Beef tomatoes are large and good with steak.

Italian plum tomatoes are good for pasta sauces. They are the ones usually sold in tins but now often available fresh in supermarkets.

Other ingredients

You can combine almost anything to make a salad. Other standard salad ingredients include: cucumber, green, red or yellow peppers, spring onions, olives, and shredded carrot.

If you want a substantial salad try adding hard-boiled eggs, fish like tuna, cheese or ham.

Fruit such as chopped apples, pears, oranges or bananas.

Walnuts, peanuts or even a few pecan nuts, cashew nuts or almonds.

Dried fruit like a couple of tablespoons of sultanas, raisins, apricot & dates.

Cooked vegetables like potato, green beans or French beans.

VINAIGRETTE

① Preparation 1 min – Easy

INGREDIENTS
3–5 tablespoons olive oil
1 tablespoon white wine vinegar
Salt and pepper
1 teaspoon mustard (optional)
1 garlic clove (optional)

EQUIPMENT
1 screw-top jar
Garlic crusher
Set of measuring spoons

METHOD
Peel and crush the garlic into the jar. Put all the other ingredients in the screw-top jar and shake vigorously. The vinaigrette will go opaque and thick. It will keep in the fridge for three weeks.

ADDITIONS & ALTERNATIVES

Try mixing half and half ordinary and extra virgin olive oil.

Substitute sunflower oil or walnut oil for the olive oil.

Substitute lemon juice, orange juice or herb vinegar for the wine vinegar.

Try combinations of the ingredients with different salads. All combinations taste good.

TIPS

Prepared garlic is sold in tubes and jars. Just read the tube or jar for the suggested equivalent amount. It keeps for six weeks in the fridge.

Olive oils vary in taste. Extra virgin is more fruity, and interesting than ordinary olive oil but also more expensive. Different brands of extra virgin even taste different, just like different wines.

By the way, extra virgin is too good to fry in, the extra flavour just evaporates.

Good vinegars to use are white or red wine, cider or even ones that have had herbs added. Don't use malt vinegar, it is cheap but only good for chip shops, or making pickles.

BLUE CHEESE DRESSING

Enough for a big bowl of salad   ① *Preparation 5 min – Easy*

INGREDIENTS

Vinaigrette
2 tablespoons of crumbly blue cheese like Roquefort or Stilton

EQUIPMENT

Bowl
Set of measuring spoons

METHOD

Break up the cheese and stir thoroughly into the vinaigrette if you like it lumpy or beat it if you like it smooth.

TIPS

This will keep for a couple of days in a tightly sealed jar in the fridge.

AMERICAN THOUSAND ISLAND DRESSING

Enough for a big bowl of salad   ① *Preparation 10 min – Easy*

INGREDIENTS

1 tablespoon chives
1 tablespoon parsley
2 tablespoons olives, stoned or stuffed
1 tablespoon green pepper
1 cup mayonnaise
3 tablespoons tomato ketchup

EQUIPMENT

Sharp knife
Chopping board
Bowl
Set of measuring spoons
Set of measuring cups

METHOD

Wash and dry the chives and parsley. Chop the olives, green pepper, chives and parsley. Mix the mayonnaise and the ketchup. Put all the ingredients in the bowl and mix together.

Use as a dressing on sliced iceberg lettuce or eggs.

APPLE, ORANGE & CHEESE SALAD

Serves 2 to 4   ① *Preparation 7 min – Easy*

INGREDIENTS
2 oranges
2 crisp eating apples
200 g (8 oz) Edam or Gouda cheese in a piece
1 tablespoon lemon juice or juice of half a lemon

EQUIPMENT
Sharp knife
Chopping board
Serving bowl
Vegetable peeler (optional)
Set of measuring spoons

METHOD
Peel the oranges with the knife. Dig out the pips. Cut the orange into 1 cm (half-inch) cubes. Put into the bowl.

Peel the apples. Cut in half and take out the core. Cut into cubes. Put in the bowl with the orange and the lemon juice and mix together, otherwise the apple will go brown.

Peel the skin off the cheese and cut into cubes. Just before you want to serve the salad put it into the bowl with the apple and orange and mix together.

ADDITIONS & ALTERNATIVES
This is a great salad with kebabs, or grilled meat like steak or chops.

BEAN SPROUT SALAD WITH YOGHURT DRESSING

Serves 4   ① *Preparation 5 min – Easy*

INGREDIENTS
200 g pack alfalfa or other sprouted seeds
2 spring onions
1 tablespoon parsley
Small carton (142 ml or 5 fl oz) yoghurt
Salt and freshly ground pepper to taste
Bread
Green salad

EQUIPMENT
Sharp knife
Chopping board
Wooden spoon
Bowl
Set of measuring spoons

METHOD
Wash and drain the sprouts.

Clean and prepare the spring onions. Cut the root end off, trim the leaves. Peel off and discard any dried up or slimy leaves. Chop into thin slices.

Wash, drain and chop the parsley. Put the spring onions and parsley into the bowl with the yoghurt. Mix together. Season with salt and pepper. Add the sprouts. Stir the sprouts in the yoghurt mixture until they are coated.

Serve with bread and green salad.

CHEDDAR CHEESE, WALNUT, CELERY & RAISIN SALAD

Serves 4   ① *Preparation 10 min – Easy*

INGREDIENTS

200 g (8 oz) Cheddar cheese
2 sticks celery
1 or 2 eating apples
Few mint leaves
4 tablespoons Greek yoghurt
3 tablespoons raisins
About 10 shelled walnuts, chopped

EQUIPMENT

Sharp knife
Chopping board
Small bowl
Set of measuring spoons

METHOD

Cut the cheese into cubes. Wash and clean the celery. Cut off the ends and leaves. Cut into slices. Peel and cube the apples, discarding the core and seeds. Cut the mint into tiny bits and mix in the bowl together with the yoghurt. Put the cheese, celery, apples, raisins and walnuts into the bowl. Stir it round so the ingredients are covered in the yoghurt. If it looks too dry put in more yoghurt.

ADDITIONS & ALTERNATIVES

Try using vinaigrette instead of the yoghurt and mint. There's a recipe for vinaigrette on page 63.

WATERMELON & FETA CHEESE SALAD

Serves 4 to 6   ① *Preparation 5 min – Easy*

INGREDIENTS
1 small to medium watermelon (about 2 kg or 4 lbs)
200 g (8 oz) pack Feta cheese

EQUIPMENT
Sharp knife
Chopping board
Bowl

METHOD
Cut the watermelon into large slices. Peel off the green skin and the pale inner layer. Cut the flesh into large chunks. Put in a bowl.

Chop the Feta cheese into small chunks. Put on top of the watermelon and serve.

ADDITIONS & ALTERNATIVES
Try drained cottage cheese instead of Feta.

TIPS
Ripe watermelon should be red with black seeds (unless they are seedless).

CHICK PEA SALAD

Serves 2 to 4 but good for parties   ⏲ *Preparation 15 min – Easy*

INGREDIENTS
2 × 400 g tins or jars of chick peas
Small bunch coriander or parsley
2 tablespoons olive oil
1 tablespoon lemon juice
Pitta bread

EQUIPMENT
Tin opener
Bowl
Sharp knife
Chopping board
Set of measuring spoons
Wooden spoon

METHOD
Open the tins or jars of chick peas. Drain. Put in the bowl. Wash and chop the coriander or parsley. Put the coriander, oil and lemon juice in with the chick peas. Mix together.

Serve with other salads and pitta bread.

ADDITIONS & ALTERNATIVES
Add sweet corn, chopped up sweet red peppers, onions or olives.

If you are going to make a lot of this for a party it is easy to cook the chick peas. There are full instructions in the 'How to' chapter.

GARLIC SAUSAGE & AVOCADO SALAD

*Serves 1 or 2 depending on
what you eat it with*   ① *Preparation 5 min – Easy*

INGREDIENTS
1 ripe avocado
200 g (8 oz) garlic sausage in a lump, not sliced up
1 small carton (142 ml or 5 fl oz) of natural unsweetened
   Greek yoghurt
Bread or toast
Green salad

EQUIPMENT
Sharp knife
Chopping board
Spoon
Small bowl

METHOD
Cut the avocado in half and take out the stone. Peel it and cut into
1 cm (half-inch) cubes. If it is really hard or horribly brown, throw
it away and eat something else, like garlic sausage sandwich.

   Peel and cut the garlic sausage into 1 cm (half-inch) cubes. Put
the yoghurt in the bowl. Add the garlic sausage and the avocado.

   Serve with toast, bread, lettuce or green salad.

ADDITIONS & ALTERNATIVES
Add chopped parsley or chopped mint for a different flavour.

   Use tinned frankfurters chopped up instead of garlic sausage.

TIPS
Ripe avocados are green but not hard; they give a little at the end
when gently pressed.

GREEK SALAD

Serves 2   ⏱ *Preparation 5 min – Easy*

INGREDIENTS
100 g (4 oz) pack of Feta cheese
1 large ripe tomato
$\frac{1}{2}$ cucumber
100 g (4 oz) black olives
1 tablespoon lemon juice
2 tablespoons olive oil

EQUIPMENT
Sharp knife
Chopping board
Serving dish
Set of measuring spoons

METHOD
Cut the Feta cheese into chunks. Cut the tomato into chunks. Cut the cucumber into chunks. Put the cheese, tomato, cucumber and olives in a dish. Pour the oil and lemon juice over the top. Stir and serve.

BREAD & TOMATO SALAD

Serves 6   ⏲ *Preparation 5 min – Easy*

INGREDIENTS
2 tablespoons parsley
2 cloves garlic
6 large ripe tomatoes
1 small cucumber
3 tablespoons extra virgin olive oil
1 tablespoon lemon juice
1 loaf of ciabatta Italian bread or a French stick

EQUIPMENT
Set of measuring spoons
Sharp knife
Chopping board
Wooden spoon
Bowl

METHOD
Wash, drain and chop the parsley. Peel and chop the garlic. Wash and coarsely chop the tomatoes. Wash, peel and dice the cucumber. Put the cucumber, tomato, parsley, garlic, olive oil and lemon juice into the bowl. Mix round. Break the bread into bite-sized chunks. Add to the bowl. Stir.

ADDITIONS & ALTERNATIVES
Try fresh coriander leaves instead of the parsley.
    Add chopped anchovies.
    Add a drained tin of tuna.
    Add olives.

MOZZARELLA SALAD

Serves 2   ⏱ *Preparation 5 min – Easy*

INGREDIENTS
100g packet of Mozzarella cheese
1 or 2 (very large) beef tomatoes
1 Spanish onion
Freshly ground pepper to taste
2 tablespoons extra virgin olive oil
Fresh basil leaves (optional)
French bread

EQUIPMENT
Sharp knife
Chopping board
Set of measuring spoons

METHOD
Mozzarella cheese is sold in lumps in plastic bags. It is the mild stringy cheese used on top of pizza. Open the pack and drain off the fluid. Slice the cheese.

Wash and slice the tomatoes. Cut the top and bottom off the onion, peel, and slice into rings. Arrange the ingredients on a plate, overlapping the slices. Grind black pepper over the salad, and dribble the olive oil over the salad.

Eat with fresh crusty French bread.

ADDITIONS & ALTERNATIVES
Add fresh basil leaves.
Add some stoned olives.

SALAD NIÇOISE

Serves 4 as an accompaniment   ⏱ *Preparation 5 min,*
Cooking 5–7 min – Easy

INGREDIENTS
250 g (9 oz) French beans
1 crisp lettuce (Iceberg or Webb's Wonderful)
Vinaigrette (see recipe on page 63)

some or all of the following:
2 tomatoes
2 hard-boiled eggs
4 anchovies
1 cup olives (green or black, plain or stuffed)
Onion rings

EQUIPMENT
Sharp knife
Chopping board
Bowl
Set of measuring cups

METHOD
Wash the beans and chop into inch lengths. Boil for 5–7 minutes, drain and throw into cold water, and leave to cool.

Wash, dry and chop the lettuce. Toss the beans in vinaigrette. Put in the bottom of a bowl. Put the lettuce on top. Arrange on top quartered tomatoes, quartered hard-boiled eggs, anchovies and olives and onion rings.

Just before serving pour some more vinaigrette on top.

WALDORF SALAD

Serves 2   ① *Preparation 5 min – Easy*

INGREDIENTS

2 sticks of celery

2 eating apples

Small bunch of seedless grapes (about 200 g or 8 oz)

100 g packet of chopped walnuts or pecan nuts

1 cup of mayonnaise

EQUIPMENT

Sharp knife

Chopping board

Bowl

Spoon

Set of measuring cups

METHOD

Clean and chop the celery. Wash and cut the apples into small dice. Discard the pips and apple core. Mix all the ingredients in the bowl.

COLESLAW

Makes a lot   ⏱ *Preparation 7 min – Easy*

INGREDIENTS
Half a white cabbage
3 carrots
3 or more tablespoons mayonnaise
Salt and freshly ground pepper to taste

EQUIPMENT
Sharp knife
Chopping board
Vegetable peeler
Grater
Bowl
Set of measuring spoons

METHOD
Cut the cabbage into really, really thin slices. Then cut it across, otherwise the bits tend to be a bit long. Alternatively, use a grater and shred the cabbage.

Cut the top, leaves and pointed end off the carrots and discard. Peel them. Grate them up. Mix with the cabbage in the bowl. Add 3 tablespoons of mayonnaise. Mix it thoroughly. If it is not enough to coat the cabbage and carrot add some more. Season to taste.

ADDITIONS & ALTERNATIVES
Use red cabbage instead of white.

Clean and chop 2 sticks of celery and add them.

Add half a cup of raisins

Add a handful of peanuts or other nuts. Use unsalted ones and chop roughly.

Use yoghurt instead of some or all the mayonnaise.

SPINACH, MUSHROOM & BACON SALAD

Serves 4 as an accompaniment   ⏱ *Preparation 5 min,*
Cooking 6 min – Easy

INGREDIENTS
500 g (1 lb) of fresh spinach (small leaves are best)
100–200 g (4 to 8 oz) of mushrooms, about 20 in number
6 rashers of streaky bacon
Vinaigrette (see page 63)

EQUIPMENT
Sharp knife
Chopping board
Frying-pan
Kitchen paper

METHOD
Cut the bacon into small pieces. Fry in the pan until crispy. Take the bacon out of the pan and leave to stand on kitchen paper.

Wipe the mushrooms with a piece of paper. Don't wash them because they will go slimy. Cut the bottom of the stalks off. Slice the mushrooms.

Get the spinach and pull the stalks off. It will pull the main vein from the middle of the leaf. Wash the spinach. Dry it and then shred. Put the spinach in a bowl, then the mushrooms then the bacon.

Just before you serve it top off with vinaigrette.

ADDITIONS & ALTERNATIVES
Substitute croutons for bacon. Croutons are crisp fried cubes of bread. Cut some small 1 cm cubes of bread. Put some oil in a frying-pan with a crushed clove of garlic (optional). Heat the oil. Drop in the bread and stir. It should be cooked in two minutes.

PASTA SALAD

Serves 2 or more   ① *Preparation 10 min, Cooking 15 min*
– Moderate

INGREDIENTS
Half a 250 g pack of small to medium-sized dried pasta shapes
   Swirls, shells, coloured or plain are suitable (About 2–3 cups)
2 tablespoons olive oil
1 green or red sweet pepper

EQUIPMENT
Saucepan
Set of measuring cups
Sieve or colander to drain the pasta
Bowl
Set of measuring spoons
Sharp knife
Chopping board

METHOD
Cook the pasta. If you have a problem with this there are full instructions in the 'How to' chapter. Read the packet for the cooking time and instructions for the pasta. Cook in at least a pint of boiling water. Drain the pasta.

Throw the pasta into the bowl with the oil and mix it up while it is still hot. This stops the pasta sticking together in a cold congealed mass. It also stops all the water from evaporating and stops it from drying up.

Meanwhile wash and dry the green or red pepper. Cut it open and throw away the seeds, stalk and top. Cut into small pieces. Put in with the pasta.

ADDITIONS & ALTERNATIVES

Add a small can of drained sweet corn, half an onion chopped small, or about 20 small mushrooms, wiped and sliced.

PASTA SALAD WITH AVOCADO

Serves 2 or more   ① *Preparation 10 min,*
Cooking 15 min – Moderate

INGREDIENTS

Half a 250 g pack of small to medium-sized dried pasta shapes
    Swirls, shells, coloured or plain are suitable (About 2–3 cups)
1 tablespoon olive oil
250 g (9 oz) pack of bacon
1 eating apple
1 ripe avocado
2 teaspoon lemon juice
Lettuce

EQUIPMENT

Saucepan
Set of measuring cups
Sieve or colander
Bowl
Set of measuring spoons
Grill
Sharp knife
Chopping board

METHOD

Read the pasta packet for the cooking time. For most sorts it is about 10 to 15 minutes. Cook the pasta. If you have a problem with this there are full instructions in the 'How to' chapter. Drain the pasta.

Throw the pasta into the bowl with the oil and mix it up while it is still hot. This stops the pasta sticking together into a cold congealed mass. It also stops all the water from evaporating and stops the pasta from drying up.

Meanwhile grill the bacon. When it is cooked and crispy, chop it up. Wash the apple. Cut the core and pips out and discard. Cut into small pieces. Cut the avocado in half and remove the stone. Peel the skin off the avocado. Cut the avocado into bits. Put the bacon, apple and avocado in with the pasta. Add the lemon juice. Stir everything round.

Serve with lettuce.

ADDITIONS & ALTERNATIVES

Add any of the following:

1 small can of drained sweet corn
$\frac{1}{2}$ onion chopped small
100 g (4 oz) of mushrooms, wiped and sliced
150 g olives
2 chopped frankfurters

POTATO SALAD

Serves 2 ① *Preparation 5 min, Cooking 20 min – Easy*

INGREDIENTS
500 g (1 lb) new potatoes
4 spring onions
3 or 4 tablespoons mayonnaise

EQUIPMENT
Sharp knife
Chopping board
Saucepan
Wooden spoon
Set of measuring spoons

METHOD
Clean the potatoes. Scrape off any eyes or shoots. Don't peel them unless you really think they need it. Put them in the pan with water to cover them. Boil for about 15 to 20 minutes. How to tell if potatoes are done: get a fork and stick it into a potato. If it goes in easily they are just right. If they completely fall apart they are overcooked. If they are still hard, give them a couple of minutes more then test again.

Meanwhile cut the top and bottom off the spring onions. Take off the outer leaf and discard any slimy bits. Give the spring onions a wash and cut them into fine rings. Cut up the potatoes. Mix the potatoes, spring onions and mayonnaise.

ADDITIONS & ALTERNATIVES
New potatoes are small, hard and solid.

Try designer potatoes like Pink Fir Apple or Charlotte's.

Add a tablespoon of chopped parsley.

The salad can be pepped up with either a chopped hard-boiled egg, 3 chopped gherkins, or 2 tablespoons of capers.

TABBOULEH

Serves 4   ℗ *Preparation 5 min plus an hour*
                             for the bulgar to soak – Easy

INGREDIENTS
250 g bulgar wheat (about 2 cups)
1 bunch of parsley
3 medium tomatoes, red and ripe
2 tablespoons of olive oil
1 tablespoon of lemon juice
Pitta bread

EQUIPMENT
Set of measuring cups
Sharp knife
Chopping board
Sieve
Bowl
Set of measuring spoons

METHOD
Wash the bulgar and soak for one hour in cold water. The bulgar will get soft and expand.

Meanwhile wash, dry and chop the parsley. Wash the tomatoes. Chop the tomatoes in half and use your finger to get the seeds out. Then chop them into very small cubes.

Drain the bulgar in a sieve. It should be squeezed to remove the excess water. This can be done by putting kitchen paper on top of the bulgar and pressing with the heel of the hand. Put the bulgar, the chopped tomatoes and parsley into a bowl. Mix them up with the lemon juice and olive oil.

Serve with pitta bread.

83

ADDITIONS & ALTERNATIVES

Substitute coriander for the parsley.

Try this with hummus, taramasalata or lamb kebabs.

THREE BEAN SALAD

Serves 4 to 6   ⏲ *Preparation 5 min – Easy*

INGREDIENTS

400 g tin red kidney beans
400 g tin chick peas
400 g tin baked beans
Few sprigs of parsley
2 tablespoons of oil
1 tablespoon of lemon juice, or juice of half a lemon

EQUIPMENT

Tin opener
Bowl
Sharp knife
Chopping board
Set of measuring spoons
Wooden spoon

METHOD

Open the tin of baked beans. Pour them into the bowl. Open the chick peas and the red kidney beans. Drain off the fluid. Put the beans and chick peas into the bowl.

Chop up the parsley. Put into the bowl together with the oil and lemon juice. Mix it all together. Keep in the fridge until ready to eat.

ADDITIONS & ALTERNATIVES

Use a tin of butter beans instead of the kidney beans or flageolet beans instead of the chick peas.

ROSE COCO BEAN SALAD

Serves 4   ① *Preparation 10 min and 2 hours waiting for
the beans to swell up, Cooking 150 min – Moderate*

INGREDIENTS
250 g dried rose coco (Borlotti) beans (about 1⅓ cups)
2 carrots
3 tablespoons sultanas
at least 2 tablespoons vinaigrette (see recipe on page 63)
1 small onion (optional)

EQUIPMENT
Set of measuring cups
Bowl
Saucepan
Vegetable peeler
Sharp knife
Chopping board
Grater
Set of measuring spoons
Wooden spoon

METHOD
Wash the beans. Put the beans in the bowl. Pour boiling water on top
of them, and cover with about 5 cm (2 inches) of water. Leave them
for 1–2 hours to swell up. Then wash the rose coco beans and put in
the saucepan with at least a pint of fresh water. Bring to the boil and
boil vigorously for 10 minutes. Turn down the heat and simmer till
they are soft. This should take about two and a half hours. Add more
water if it runs low. Let the beans cool down.

　　　Wash and peel the carrots. Cut off the top and bottom ends.
Grate the carrots. Put the rose coco beans, grated carrot, sultana
and vinaigrette in the bowl and mix together.

85

ADDITIONS & ALTERNATIVES

Try the orange vinaigrette made with orange juice instead of vinegar.

This is good with pitta bread and hummus.

TIPS

You can make this some time before you want to eat it. The knack is to boil the beans, then keep them going gently, adding more water when it gets a bit low. The only real difficulty is that you may get distracted, they boil dry, and the pan gets ruined.

EGGS

BOILED EGG

Serves 1 or 2   ① *Preparation 2 min, Cooking 3 min – Easy*

INGREDIENTS
2 eggs
1 teaspoon vinegar

EQUIPMENT
Saucepan

METHOD
This recipe gives you boiled eggs which have a cooked white and a runny hot yolk. Put the eggs in the pan and cover with water. Add a teaspoon of vinegar. Use a stopwatch if you have one.

Bring the water to the boil. Start timing from when the water reaches boiling point. Wait three minutes. Take the eggs out of the water. Eat immediately.

Serve with salt and pepper and toast.

ADDITIONS & ALTERNATIVES
If you like your egg yolks more solid, cook for an extra minute.

Hard-boiled eggs should be cooked for about ten minutes and then cooled off in water before trying to handle them.

TIPS
Use eggs at room temperature. Do not keep eggs in the fridge.

EGG MAYONNAISE

Serves 2   ① *Preparation 3 min, Cooking 10 min – Easy*

INGREDIENTS
3 eggs
1 teaspoon vinegar
2 tablespoons mayonnaise
Salt and freshly ground pepper to taste

EQUIPMENT
Saucepan
Set of measuring spoons
Sharp knife
Chopping board
Bowl
Fork

METHOD
Put the eggs in the pan and cover with water. Add a teaspoon of vinegar. Bring the water to the boil. Cook for about ten minutes and then cool off in water before trying to handle them.

Peel the shell off the eggs and cut in half. Separate the yolks from the whites. Mash the yolk in the bowl. Chop the whites and add to the yolks. Mix the eggs with the mayonnaise.

Add salt and pepper to taste.

ADDITIONS & ALTERNATIVES
Add 2 chopped spring onions.

Add 1 chopped small gherkin.

TIPS
Use eggs at room temperature. There is no need to keep eggs in the fridge.

SCRAMBLED EGG

Serves 1   ① *Preparation 1 min, Cooking 2 min – Easy*

INGREDIENTS
2 eggs
1 tablespoon butter
1 piece buttered toast
Salt and pepper

EQUIPMENT
Set of measuring spoons
Saucepan
Wooden spoon

METHOD
Put a piece of buttered toast on a plate. Put the lump of butter in a small pan and let the butter melt over a medium heat. Break the eggs into the pan. Add some salt and pepper. Stir the eggs to stop it sticking to the bottom of the pan and to scramble. The egg will cook within a couple of minutes. When the eggs are still moist turn them out on to the toast. Eat while hot.

Do not overcook the eggs as they end up like rubber.

ADDITIONS & ALTERNATIVES
Add bacon.

A stunning breakfast for two involves a small packet of smoked salmon trout. Cut it into pieces. Make two bits of buttered toast. Make a double quantity of scrambled eggs. Distribute on the toast. Scatter the smoked salmon trout bits on the top. Serve with coffee, fresh orange juice, champagne, or Bloody Marys.

FRIED EGG

Serves 2   ① *Preparation 1 min, Cooking 2 min – Easy*

INGREDIENTS
2 eggs
Oil

EQUIPMENT
2 cups
Frying-pan
Slotted egg slice

METHOD
Break an egg into each cup. Fish out any bits of shell which have got mixed up with it.

How do you like your eggs? Sunny side up or over easy?

Over easy: heat the oil in the frying-pan. Pour the eggs into the pan. When the white has gone solid, use the spatula to free up the eggs gently from the base of the pan. Flip the eggs over and cook for another thirty seconds.

Sunny side up: this is like over easy, except that when the white starts to cook, flick the hot oil over the yolk. The top will turn white. Free up from the bottom of the pan and serve.

ADDITIONS & ALTERNATIVES
Serve with grilled bacon or sausages, or bread and butter.

When you get better at this you can break the egg directly into the pan. It is, however, somewhat more dangerous to try and fish out bits of shell from hot oil.

The traditional way to cook eggs is to use the fat from the sausages and bacon you have already cooked.

The ultimate cholesterol-high breakfast would include fried bread and fried tomatoes.

OMELETTE

Serves 1 ⓘ *Preparation 3 min, Cooking 1 min – Easy*

INGREDIENTS
2 fresh eggs at room temperature
1 tablespoon butter
Pepper

EQUIPMENT
Bowl
Fork
Frying-pan
Wooden spoon

METHOD
Break the eggs into a bowl and pick out any bits of shell. Add the pepper and mix the eggs up with a fork. (Don't add salt to the uncooked eggs because it makes the omelette tough.)

Heat some butter to grease the bottom of a thick frying-pan. Don't let it get too hot and burn the butter. Pour in the eggs and let them spread. Shake the pan gently and gently stir the eggs with a wooden spoon. In a minute or so the omelette is cooked and can be slid on to a plate.

ADDITIONS & ALTERNATIVES
Add 1 tablespoon of cream, milk or cheese to the mixture.

Add mixed herbs or paprika pepper.

You can fill the omelette with warmed bits of chopped ham, chicken, or cooked mushrooms.

Serve with salad.

TIPS
Let the eggs warm up to room temperature before putting them in the pan. Have the pan hot enough to cook the eggs.

ITALIAN MEATY OMELETTE

Serves 4   ⏲ *Preparation 5 min, Cooking 15 min – Easy*

INGREDIENTS
2 tablespoons freshly chopped parsley
10 mushrooms (about 100 g (4 oz))
Small to medium onion
100 g (4 oz) spicy sausage (salami, chorizo or pepperoni)
2 tablespoons olive oil
6 eggs
50 g (2 oz) grated Parmesan cheese (about 3 tablespoons)
Salad

EQUIPMENT
Sharp knife
Chopping board
Frying-pan
Wooden spoon
Set of measuring spoons
Bowl
Grill

METHOD
Wash, drain and chop the parsley. Wipe and chop the mushrooms in half. Peel and chop the onion. Slice the sausage. Put the oil in the frying-pan. Cook the spicy sausage, onion and mushrooms together for a couple of minutes, giving them the odd stir.

Meanwhile, break the eggs into a bowl and pick out any bits of shell. Add the Parmesan and parsley and mix the eggs up with a fork. Add the egg mixture to the frying-pan, and cook on moderate heat for about five minutes.

Put it under a grill for about three minutes to finish it off. It should go golden on top. Cut into triangular segments.

Serve with salad.

ADDITIONS & ALTERNATIVES

Substitute half a bunch of spring onions for the onion.

Try other cheeses: 50g (2 oz or 1 cup) of grated Cheddar or similar would do.

Try adding vegetables like courgettes or onions. Just wash or peel, chop and fry in a tablespoon of butter for three minutes.

Use chopped smoked sausage or hot dogs instead of spicy sausage.

SPANISH OMELETTE

Serves 4   *① Preparation 5 min, Cooking 20 min – Easy*

INGREDIENTS
2 large potatoes
1 onion
4 eggs
Freshly ground pepper to taste
2 tablespoons olive oil

EQUIPMENT
Vegetable peeler
Sharp knife
Chopping board
Saucepan
Colander or sieve
Bowl
Fork
Frying-pan
Set of measuring spoons
Wooden spoon
Grill

METHOD

Peel the potatoes. Chop into 1 cm (half-inch) cubes. Boil for about 5 minutes, checking that they do not fall apart. Drain the potato. Peel and chop the onion.

Meanwhile, break the eggs into a bowl and pick out any bits of shell. Add the pepper and mix the eggs up with a fork. Heat the oil in the frying-pan. Fry the onion and the potato. Stir from time to time. When they are golden add the eggs and turn the heat down really low. The omelette should be about 2–3 cm (1 inch) thick. Put a lid on the pan and leave it for at least ten minutes.

To brown the top put it under a grill for a couple of minutes to finish it off. When it is cooked the eggs will not be runny. Cut it into triangular pieces.

ADDITIONS & ALTERNATIVES

Try other fillings of meat and vegetables, cooking them first. Broccoli, peas, mushrooms, garlic sausage and cooked ham work well. Or add chopped cooked streaky bacon to the recipe.

POACHED EGGS ON TOAST

Serves 1   ① *Preparation 1 min, Cooking 2 to 3 min*
          – Potentially a fiddle but the best version of solo eggs

INGREDIENTS

2 eggs, as fresh as possible
1 teaspoon of vinegar
1 slice of buttered toast

EQUIPMENT
2 cups
Saucepan
Spoon with holes in it to drain the eggs
Fork to let the water out

METHOD
Put the buttered toast on a plate. Use eggs that have not been kept in the fridge. Break one egg into each cup. Fish out any bits of shell which have got mixed up with it. Put at least a pint of water and the teaspoon of vinegar in the pan and bring to the boil. Stir the boiling water. Turn down the water so it is simmering (not boiling violently). Slide the eggs out of the cup into the water. They will hold together, though there may be some white froth which needs to be scooped off the surface. If the eggs appear to stick to the pan, wait till they are fairly well cooked before trying to dislodge them.

The eggs will be cooked when the white is solid and the yolk runny. This takes about two or three minutes. Fish the eggs out with the spoon. Let out any water which has become trapped in pockets of white with the fork. If the white is still runny put it back in the boiling water and cook for a little longer. Put the cooked eggs on the toast.

ADDITIONS & ALTERNATIVES
Serve with baked beans on toast.

There is a special pan which can poach four eggs at a time. Put the water in the bottom, grease the cups with butter, put the eggs in the indentations, and cook for about three minutes.

WALNUT & LEEK QUICHE

Serves 6 ⓘ *Preparation 15 min, Cooking 45 min*
– Cooking the pastry in two stages is a bit of a fiddle,
but otherwise no problem

INGREDIENTS
450 g pack pre-rolled frozen shortcrust pastry
100 g (4 oz) grated Cheddar cheese, about 2 cups
3 eggs
2 tablespoons milk
Salt and pepper
4 to 6 slender to medium leeks (about 500g or 1 lb)
1 tablespoon butter
100 g (4 oz) walnut halves (about 20)

EQUIPMENT
Round ovenproof dish about 24 cm (9.5 inches) across
Greaseproof paper
1 pack dried beans to hold the pastry down
Grater
Set of measuring cups
Bowl
Set of measuring spoons
Sharp knife
Chopping board
Wooden spoon

METHOD
Make sure the pastry is thawed. Check the packet for times, but generally about four hours in the fridge.

Lightly grease the dish. Unroll the pastry and place in the dish. Pastry is fairly flexible so you can push it into place. If it tears, patch it with a spare bit, moistening with water to make sure it sticks. Prick the bottom of the pastry with a fork at least five times to let steam out. Cut a piece of greaseproof paper to fit and press gently on to the pastry. Fill the bottom with a layer of cheap dried beans, for instance butter beans. Cook the pastry case at 200°C, 400°F, Gas mark 6 for 10 to 15 minutes until the top edges go golden.

Take the pastry case out of the oven. Wait for it to cool then take out the beans and greaseproof paper.

Meanwhile grate the cheese. Break the eggs into a bowl and pick out any bits of shell. Add the milk, salt and pepper. Mix with a fork.

Clean the leeks. First take off the outer leaves, cut the roots off and trim the top. Split the leeks in half lengthways. Hold the leeks under running water and wash any grit out. Shake them dry. Cut into 1 cm (half-inch) slices.

Put the butter in the pan and melt over a medium heat. Put the leeks in and cook for about three minutes to soften them. Take off the heat.

Put some walnuts on the pastry case. Use the broken ones. Spread the leeks over the walnuts. Scatter the cheese on top. Place the best walnut halves on the cheese. Pour the egg mixture on top.

Cook in a preheated oven at 170°C, 325°F, Gas mark 3 for about 20 to 30 minutes till set and golden brown.

Eat hot or cold.

ADDITIONS & ALTERNATIVES

On leeks: don't use really thick ones as they are tougher.

Try other sorts of cheese like Gouda or even crumbled blue cheese half and half with cheddar.

Various combinations of ingredients work; try chopped up cooked ham and mushroom. Chop the mushrooms in half and fry for one minute in a tablespoon of butter, then put in the pastry case.

BACON & TOMATO QUICHE

Serves 6   ① *Preparation 15 min, Cooking 45 min*
Cooking the pastry in two stages is a bit of a fiddle,
but otherwise no problem

INGREDIENTS

Use the previous recipe but substitute the leek and walnuts with:
8 rashers bacon cooked and chopped
2 medium tomatoes

METHOD

Make the pastry case as in the previous recipe.

Chop up the bacon into 2.5 cm (1 inch) lengths. Fry gently for a couple of minutes to get some of the fat off. Put the bacon in the bottom of the pastry case.

Wash and slice the tomatoes. Keep a couple of slices for decoration and put the rest in with the bacon. Add the cheese followed by the reserved tomato slices. Top with the egg mixture. Cook in a preheated oven at 170°C, 325°F, Gas mark 3 for about 20 to 30 minutes till set and golden brown.

ADDITIONS & ALTERNATIVES

You can substitute a small carton (142 ml or 5 fl oz) of single cream for one of the eggs and the milk.

BIG BREAKFAST PIE

Serves 4–6   ① *Preparation 15 min, Cooking 45 min – Easy*

INGREDIENTS

450 g pack of pre-rolled frozen shortcrust pastry
100 g (4 oz) grated Cheddar cheese, about 2 cups
3 eggs
2 tablespoons milk

Salt and pepper
4 frankfurters (about 100–150 g)
2 large onions
1 tablespoon butter

EQUIPMENT
Round ovenproof dish about 24 cm (9.5 inches) across
1 pack dried beans to hold the pastry down
Greaseproof paper
Grater
Set of measuring cups
Bowl
Set of measuring spoons
Sharp knife
Chopping board
Frying-pan
Wooden spoon

METHOD
Thaw the pastry according to the instructions on the packet. Four hours in the fridge seems typical. Make the pastry case according to the previous Quiche recipe.

Meanwhile grate the cheese. Break the eggs into a bowl and pick out any bits of shell. Add the milk, salt and pepper. Mix round with a fork.

Open the packet of frankfurters. Chop into 2.5 cm (1 inch) lengths. Peel and chop the onions. Put the butter in the frying-pan and heat over a moderate heat. Fry the onion for about three minutes till it is golden, stirring to stop it sticking. Spread the frankfurters and onions over the bottom of the pastry case. Scatter the cheese on top. Pour the egg mixture on top. Cook in a preheated oven at 170°C, 325°F, Gas mark 3 for about 20 to 30 minutes till set and golden brown.

This can be eaten hot or cold.

CHICKEN

CAJUN CHICKEN

Serves 2   ⏱ *Preparation 3 min, Cooking 20 min – Easy*

INGREDIENTS
2 chicken breasts
2 tablespoons Cajun Seasoning
1 or 2 tablespoons butter
Salad or rice to serve

EQUIPMENT
Set of measuring spoons
Frying-pan
Wooden spoon

DEFROSTING
Make sure frozen chicken is completely thawed before use. This means leaving it in the fridge overnight, or out of the fridge, covered, for six hours.

METHOD
Rub the chicken breasts with the Cajun seasoning. Melt the butter in the frying-pan. Gently fry the chicken, turning from time to time. Cook for about 15 to 20 minutes. It is normal for the breast to end up quite dark.

Serve with salad or rice.

CHICKEN BOURSIN & BACON

Serves 1 ① *Preparation 3 min, Cooking 25 to 30 min – Easy*

INGREDIENTS
1 chicken breast
16 g individual portion boursin cheese
1 rasher bacon

EQUIPMENT
Ovenproof dish
Aluminium foil

DEFROSTING
Make sure frozen chicken is completely thawed before use. This means leaving it in the fridge overnight, or out of the fridge, covered, for six hours.

METHOD
Get the chicken breast. If it has skin on, loosen it and spread the cheese between the skin and the meat. Otherwise just spread it on the breast. Put the chicken breast in the ovenproof dish. Put a rasher of bacon on the chicken breast. Cover the dish with foil.

Put into a preheated oven at 180°C, 350°F, Gas mark 4 for 20 minutes. Carefully take the foil off and cook for a further 5 to 10 minutes till browned.

ADDITIONS & ALTERNATIVES
Omit the bacon.
Serve with green salad.

CASSEROLE OF CHICKEN WITH BACON & MUSHROOM

Serves 4   ① *Preparation 7 min, Cooking 65 min – Easy*

INGREDIENTS
200 g (8 oz) button mushrooms (approximately 20)
1 onion
2 tablespoons butter
4 rashers bacon
Salt and pepper to taste
4 chicken quarters or other equivalent chicken pieces
1 stock cube

EQUIPMENT
Sharp knife
Chopping board
Frying-pan
Set of measuring spoons
Wooden spoon
Casserole with lid
Set of measuring cups

DEFROSTING
Make sure frozen chicken is completely thawed before use. This means leaving it in the fridge overnight, or out of the fridge, covered, for six hours.

METHOD
Wipe and slice the mushrooms. Peel and chop the onion. Put 1 tablespoon of butter in the frying-pan and heat over a moderate heat. Fry the onion and mushrooms for about three minutes, stirring to stop them sticking. Remove from heat. Chop the bacon into 2.5 cm (1 inch) pieces. Stir in the bacon, salt and pepper.

Put the chicken quarters in the casserole. Pour the mixture on top. Add the other tablespoon of butter. Add a stock cube and a cup of water. Put lid on the casserole. Cook in a preheated oven for one hour at 180°C, 350°F, Gas mark 4.

ADDITIONS & ALTERNATIVES
Serve with rice or vegetables.

CHICKEN BREASTS WITH LEMON

Serves 2　　　① *Preparation 3 min, Cooking 25 to 30 min – Easy*

INGREDIENTS
1 lemon
2 chicken breasts
1 tablespoon oil or butter
Pepper

EQUIPMENT
Sharp knife
Chopping board
Ovenproof dish
Aluminium foil
Set of measuring spoons

DEFROSTING
Make sure frozen chicken is completely thawed before use. This means leaving it in the fridge overnight, or out of the fridge, covered, for six hours.

METHOD
Wash and slice the lemon. Put the chicken breast in the ovenproof dish. Put the oil or butter on the chicken breast. Put the lemon slices on top and season with pepper. Cover the dish with foil.

Put into a preheated oven at 180°C, 350°F, Gas mark 4 for 20 minutes. Carefully take the foil off and cook for a further 5 to 10 minutes.

ADDITIONS & ALTERNATIVES
Serve with green salad.
Use chicken quarters.
Add half a glass of white wine.

CIDER CHICKEN

Serves 4   ① *Preparation 10 min, Cooking 60 min – Easy*

INGREDIENTS
2 large apples
2 large leeks
4 chicken quarters
1 small bottle cider (250 ml or ½ pint)
Salt and pepper
Rice or potatoes

EQUIPMENT
Sharp knife
Chopping board
Casserole dish

DEFROSTING
Make sure frozen chicken is completely thawed before use. This means leaving it in the fridge overnight, or out of the fridge, covered, for six hours.

METHOD
Peel the apples. Remove the core and seeds and chop.

Clean the leeks. First take off the outer leaves, cut the roots off and trim the top. Split the leeks in half lengthways. Hold the leeks under running water and wash any grit out. Shake them dry. Cut into 1 cm (half-inch) slices.

Put the chicken pieces in the casserole. Add the leeks and the apples. Pour the cider on top and season with salt and pepper. Put the lid on the casserole. Cook in a preheated oven at 180°C, 350°F, Gas mark 4 for an hour.

Serve with rice or potatoes.

CHICKEN POT STEW

Serves 4 ⏲ *Preparation 5 min, Cooking 3 hours – Easy*

INGREDIENTS
2 rashers bacon
4 medium potatoes
1 medium onion
4 chicken quarters
500g (1 lb) sausages
250g dried split green peas (half a packet or about $1\frac{1}{4}$ cups)
1 litre water (about 2 pints or 4 cups)
Salt and pepper

EQUIPMENT
Sharp knife
Chopping board
Casserole with lid
Set of measuring cups

DEFROSTING
Make sure frozen chicken is completely thawed before use. This means leaving it in the fridge overnight, or out of the fridge, covered, for six hours.

METHOD
Cut the bacon slices in half. Peel the potatoes and chop into quarters. Peel and slice the onion. Put all the ingredients in the casserole. Put the lid on. Cook in an oven for three hours at 140°C, 275°F, Gas mark 1.

CHICKEN VEGETABLE CASSEROLE

Serves 4   ① *Preparation 15 min, Cooking 90 min – Easy*

INGREDIENTS
3 large potatoes
3 or 4 carrots
1 large onion
10 mushrooms (about 100 g or 4 oz) (optional)
8 to 12 chicken pieces (thigh, drumstick or small breasts)
1 tablespoon mixed herbs
1 chicken stock cube
Salt and pepper
1 glass wine (optional)

EQUIPMENT
Sharp knife
Chopping board
Casserole dish
Set of measuring spoons

DEFROSTING
Make sure frozen chicken is completely thawed before use. This means leaving it in the fridge overnight, or out of the fridge, covered, for six hours.

METHOD
Peel the potatoes, cutting away any nasty bits, and cutting out any eyes. Chop the potatoes into quarters.

Peel and chop the carrots, cutting off both ends. Peel and slice the onions. Wipe the mushrooms, and chop the end off the stalks.

Put the chicken pieces in the casserole. Add all the vegetables, herbs and stock cube. Just cover the chicken with fluid, either water or water and white wine. Season with salt and pepper. Put the lid on the casserole. Cook in a preheated oven at 170°C, 325°F, Gas mark 3 for about an hour and a half.

ADDITIONS & ALTERNATIVES

Try using small chops instead of the chicken.

Other vegetables can be used with or instead of the carrots and potatoes, like parsnip, peas and beans.

Make the sauce thicker by adding 2 tablespoons of pearl barley or soup mix.

Serve with a green vegetable or salad.

ROAST CHICKEN

Serves 4   ① *Preparation 5 min, Cooking 2 hours – Easy*

INGREDIENTS
1.5 kg (3 lb) chicken
Salt and pepper
3 rashers bacon (see method)
1 tablespoon oil

EQUIPMENT
Cast-iron casserole
or Roasting tin/Ovenproof dish
or Chicken brick
Set of measuring spoons
Set of measuring cups

DEFROSTING
If frozen, make sure the chicken is thawed and that there are no
plastic bags of giblets left inside or bits of cardboard underneath.
A 1.5 kg (3 lb) chicken takes 24 hours to defrost in the fridge or 12
hours out of it.

METHOD
Season the chicken with freshly ground pepper and salt. If you
have a cast-iron casserole (le Creuset or similar) put the chicken in
with 1 tablespoon of oil and half a cup of water and roast with the
lid on.

If you have a pottery chicken brick, just put the chicken in and
roast.

If you are using a roasting dish or ovenproof dish, just put the
chicken in with 1 tablespoon of oil and half a cup of water. Cover
the breast with 3 rashers of bacon. Cover the top with foil. Cook
for 2 hours in a preheated oven at 170°C, 325°F, Gas mark 3.

When the chicken is cooked, take it out of the oven and put it on a plate. Leave it for 5 minutes before carving.

ADDITIONS & ALTERNATIVES

Serve with roast potatoes and vegetables or salad. Put the prepared vegetables in an ovenproof dish with half a cup of oil or so. Cook at the top of the oven for at least an hour. Full instructions are in the vegetarian section.

Cranberry sauce goes well with chicken.

Put an orange cut in half in the body cavity, and sprinkle the chicken with a teaspoon of mixed Mediterranean herbs.

Add a quartered lemon and a tablespoon of fresh tarragon.

Add three small onions and a tablespoon of rosemary.

Add 10 button mushrooms, a drained 250 g (9 oz) tin of sweet chestnuts and a tablespoon of tarragon.

Try Italian roast chicken. It is very quick and easy (see p. 243).

TIPS

Stuffing can be cooked in the oven. If the packet suggests a higher temperature than you are using for the chicken then just cook it for longer.

A recipe for gravy follows, if you need it.

Our personal recommendation must be for the cast-iron casserole method. It is fairly foolproof. It also means there is lots of juice for making gravy. The casserole is very useful for other oven dishes. The ideal size is a 25 cm (10 inch) oval casserole with straight sides. It holds 4 litres (7 pints) and can take a chicken, a small leg of lamb or most beef roasts, as well as being OK for all the casserole dishes.

Club Sandwich, Chicken Curry, Coronation Chicken and Chicken Creole all use left-over cooked chicken.

GRAVY

Serves 4–6   ⏲ *Preparation 2 min, Cooking 10 min – Easy*

INGREDIENTS
2 teaspoons cornflour
2 teaspoons of gravy browning powder (e.g. Bisto)
500 ml (1 pt) water, 2 cups
1 stock cube

EQUIPMENT
Set of measuring spoons
Cup
Wooden spoon
Saucepan

METHOD
Put the cornflour and gravy browning in the cup. Add about 2 tablespoons of water a few drops at a time and stir until you get a smooth paste. If you add the water all at once it will go lumpy.

Put 500 ml (1 pt) water and the stock cube in the saucepan. Put on a medium heat and stir to dissolve. When the water is hot, but before it is boiling, continue to stir with one hand and add the cornflour mixture. Keep stirring to stop it sticking and going lumpy. As the mixture comes to the boil it will thicken. Cook for a minute or so and take off the heat.

This can be reheated when everything else is ready.

ADDITIONS & ALTERNATIVES
Add 1 tablespoon of brandy.
Add 1 glass of wine.
Add the juices from the roast with most of the fat skimmed off.

CHICKEN CREOLE

Serves 2   ① *Preparation 10 min – Easy*

INGREDIENTS
200 g (8 oz) cooked potatoes
200 g (8 oz) cooked chicken or 2 chicken quarters, about 2 cups
    when chopped
1 tablespoon mayonnaise
1 tablespoon Cajun seasoning
150 g can pitted black olives

EQUIPMENT
Ovenproof dish
Sharp knife
Chopping board
Saucepan
Tin opener
Set of measuring spoons
Set of measuring cups

DEFROSTING & COOKING
If you need to cook the chicken, make sure frozen chicken is
completely thawed before use. This means leaving the quarters in
the fridge overnight, or out of the fridge, covered, for six hours.
Then just brush with oil and cook in an ovenproof dish in the oven
for 30 minutes at 200°C, 400°F, Gas mark 6.

METHOD
Cook the potatoes if not already cooked. Clean and peel if needed.
Boil in water for about 20 minutes. Cool and cut into 1 cm (half-
inch) cubes.
    Flake or break up the chicken. Mix all the ingredients together.

ADDITIONS & ALTERNATIVES
Serve with salad.
Use a tin of potatoes instead of the cooked ones.

CHICKEN RICE BAKE

Serves 4 ⓘ *Preparation 10 min, Cooking 90 min – Easy*

INGREDIENTS
4 chicken quarters
2 medium onions
3 medium carrots
$1\frac{1}{2}$ cups of long grain or risotto rice
1 chicken stock cube
3 cups water or white wine and water

EQUIPMENT
Sharp knife
Chopping board
Casserole with lid
Set of measuring cups

METHOD
Make sure frozen chicken is completely thawed before use. This
means leaving it in the fridge overnight, or out of the fridge,
covered, for six hours.
Peel and chop the onions. Peel and chop the carrots. Put the
chicken, onion and carrot in the casserole. Add the rice. Dissolve
the stock cube in the water. Add the stock to the rice. Put the lid
on the casserole. Cook in a preheated oven at 150°C, 300°F, Gas
mark 2 for 90 minutes.

ADDITIONS & ALTERNATIVES
Serve with a green vegetable.

MOROCCAN CHICKEN

Serves 4 ① *Preparation 10 min, Cooking 50 min – Easy*

INGREDIENTS
8 chicken thighs or drumsticks
2 medium onions
2 tablespoons oil for frying
2 cloves garlic
1 teaspoon turmeric
$\frac{1}{2}$ teaspoon chilli powder
400 g tin tomatoes
2 × 400 g tins chick peas
1 lemon
1 tablespoon parsley or coriander

EQUIPMENT
Sharp knife
Chopping board
Garlic crusher
Big pan or a wok
Wooden spoon
Set of measuring spoons
Tin opener
Cup

DEFROSTING
Make sure frozen chicken is completely thawed before use. This means leaving it in the fridge overnight, or out of the fridge, covered, for six hours.

METHOD

Peel and chop the onions. Put the oil in the pan and put on a medium heat. Peel and crush the garlic into the pan. Add the onion and cook on a medium heat for 5 minutes. Stir from time to time. Add the turmeric and chilli powder. Cook for another three minutes.

Add the chicken pieces and stir round until they start to cook, are covered in the mixture and are golden, about ten minutes. Add the tin of tomatoes, mashing up if required. Open the tins of chick peas. Pour the liquid off into a cup, you may need it later. Add the chick peas to the mixture. Stir it all together and cook on a medium heat (don't burn it) for about 35 minutes. If it starts to get too dry looking, add the chick pea liquid. If this runs out use water.

Just before serving, put in the lemon juice and parsley and/or coriander.

ADDITIONS & ALTERNATIVES

Serve with warm pitta bread (sprinkle them with water and grill for a minute, till they puff up).

Try eating this with tabbouleh (page 83), an appropriate salad.

TIPS

Prepared garlic is sold in tubes and jars. Just read the tube or jar for the suggested equivalent amount. It keeps for six weeks in the fridge.

CORONATION CHICKEN

Serves 2 to 4   ⏱ *Preparation 10 min – Moderate*

INGREDIENTS

Pre-cooked chicken. Can be left over from a roast. 1 breast or 3
thighs. Can be more or less.
3 tablespoons mango chutney
¹⁄₂ cucumber
Few coriander leaves (optional)
100 g pack flaked almonds
3 tablespoons mayonnaise

EQUIPMENT

Sharp knife
Chopping board
Bowl
Set of measuring spoons

DEFROSTING & COOKING

If you need to cook the chicken, make sure frozen chicken pieces
are completely thawed before use. This means leaving them in the
fridge overnight, or out of the fridge, for six hours. Then just brush
the portions with oil and cook in an ovenproof dish in the oven for
30 minutes at 200°C, 400°F, Gas mark 6.

METHOD

Get the cooked chicken and cut it up into small pieces. This is
easier if you take it off the bone first. The bits should be about 1 cm
(half-inch) thick. This is not crucial. Size is not, in this instance,
important.

If the chutney has big lumps of mango in it take them out and
chop them up. Wash the cucumber and peel it if you like. Chop
it into little cubes. Wash and cut up the coriander leaves.

Put the chicken, almonds, coriander leaves and chutney into a bowl with the mayonnaise and mix them all together.

ADDITIONS & ALTERNATIVES
Serve with pitta bread and salad.

Use mixed fruit chutney, lime pickle or peach chutney instead of the mango chutney.

FISH

DEFROSTING

In general white fish do not need to be defrosted before cooking. Cooked prawns and salmon do. Check the details on the packet.

KIPPERS

Serves 1   ① *Preparation 2 min, Cooking 10 min – Easy*

INGREDIENTS
Pair of kippers
1 tablespoon butter

EQUIPMENT
Grill
Set of measuring spoons

METHOD
Put the kipper skin side down on the grill pan and put a couple of blobs of butter on the top. Grill for about 5 to 10 minutes depending on how thick they are.

TIPS
If you find the kippers too salty or smoky, try this trick. Before cooking, soak the kipper in hot water for a couple of minutes. Drain the kipper.

CAJUN SALMON

Serves 2   ① *Preparation 3 min, Cooking 10 min – Easy*

INGREDIENTS
2 salmon steaks about 500 g or 1 lb
2 tablespoons Cajun seasoning
1–2 tablespoons butter
Salad or rice to serve

EQUIPMENT
Frying-pan
Wooden spoon
Set of measuring spoons

DEFROSTING
Make sure frozen salmon is completely thawed before use. This means leaving it in the fridge overnight, or out of the fridge, covered, for six hours.

METHOD
Wash and drain the salmon. Rub the salmon steaks with the Cajun seasoning.

Melt the butter in the frying-pan. Fry the salmon, turning from time to time. Cook for about 10 minutes. It is normal for the fish to end up quite dark.

Serve with salad or rice.

SAVOURY SALMON CRÊPES

Serves 2 to 4   ① *Preparation 7 min – Easy*

INGREDIENTS
1 packet crêpes (ready made)
200 g (8 oz) pack smoked salmon or smoked salmon trout
250 g pot Greek yoghurt
100 g jar red lumpfish roe (optional added luxury)
1 lemon
Salad

EQUIPMENT
Sharp knife
Chopping board
Set of measuring spoons

METHOD
Separate the crêpes. Put one on a plate. Put a slice of smoked salmon on the crêpe. Roll up the crêpe. Put half a tablespoon of yoghurt on the crêpe. Put a teaspoon of lumpfish roe on the yoghurt.

Make two for each person. Serve with a slice of lemon and salad.

ADDITIONS & ALTERNATIVES
Substitute cold cooked flaked salmon for the smoked salmon,

Use Parma ham instead of the salmon. Omit the lumpfish roe, and use a chopped-up gherkin or a teaspoon of capers mixed in with the yoghurt.

SALMON BOURSIN

Serves 1   ⏱ *Preparation 3 min, Cooking 20 to 25 min – Easy*

INGREDIENTS
1 salmon steak or cutlet
½ small boursin cheese or an individual (16g) portion
1 tablespoon oil

EQUIPMENT
Baking dish
Set of measuring spoons
Aluminium foil

METHOD
Put the salmon steak in the baking dish. Spread the cheese on the salmon. Pour the oil on the top. Cover the dish with foil. Put into a preheated oven at 180°C, 350°F, Gas mark 4 for 20 minutes.

ADDITIONS & ALTERNATIVES
Serve with salad or new potatoes.
   Use salmon fillet.

PLAICE WITH WINE

Serves 4   ① *Preparation 1 min, Cooking 15 min – Easy*

INGREDIENTS
600 g pack frozen small plaice (about 5 fillets)
1 tablespoon fresh parsley
Salt and freshly ground pepper to taste
1 tablespoon butter
1 glass white wine

EQUIPMENT
Sharp knife
Chopping board
Ovenproof dish
Set of measuring spoons
Aluminium kitchen foil

METHOD
Wash the fish and drain. Wash, drain and chop the parsley. Put the
fish in the ovenproof dish. Season with salt and pepper. Put the
butter on the fish in little blobs. Pour the wine into the dish. Cover
the dish with aluminium foil. Cook in a preheated oven at 170°C,
325°F, Gas mark 3 for 20 minutes.

When ready to serve spoon the juice over the fish and garnish
with the chopped parsley.

ADDITIONS & ALTERNATIVES
Serve with new potatoes, green vegetable or salad.

Add two tablespoons of Greek yoghurt to the juice, and stir and
warm through.

FISH IN THE PAN

Serves 2   ⏲ *Preparation 1 min, Cooking 5 min – Easy*

INGREDIENTS
2 fillets of cod, hake or haddock about 500g (1 lb)
2 tablespoons olive oil
Salt and freshly ground pepper to taste

EQUIPMENT
Frying-pan
Fish slice
Set of measuring spoons

METHOD
If cooking the fish from frozen, cook more slowly to begin with. Check it is cooked through to the middle.

Put the oil in the pan and heat up. Place the fish in the pan. Fry for a couple of minutes each side. The fish is cooked when the flesh has changed colour. Season to taste.

ADDITIONS & ALTERNATIVES
Serve with salad.

Add a crushed clove of garlic to the oil.

Use butter, ground black pepper and 1 teaspoon of capers instead of the oil.

TROUT & ALMONDS

Serves 2   ① *Preparation 2 min, Cooking 10 min – Easy*

INGREDIENTS
2 rainbow trout
Salt and freshly ground pepper to taste
1 tablespoon butter
100 g pack flaked almonds
1 lemon

EQUIPMENT
Grill
Aluminium kitchen foil
Set of measuring spoons

METHOD
You can get fish with the head off. Brush butter on the outside of the fish. Cover the grill pan with tin foil. Put the fish on the grill pan. Grill for about 5 minutes.

Turn the fish over. Put more butter on. Sprinkle the flaked almonds on the fish and season with salt and pepper. Grill for about five minutes. It's OK for the skin to get quite dark.

Serve with a segment of lemon.

ADDITIONS & ALTERNATIVES
Serve with salad or new potatoes.

Put some dill inside the fish before cooking.

TIPS
Throw away the tin foil and the grill pan will still be clean.

HOT GARLIC PRAWNS

Serves 3 as a starter ① *Preparation 3 min, Cooking 10 min – Easy*

INGREDIENTS
200 g pack frozen extra large prawns
1 lemon
6 cloves garlic
2 tablespoons oil
Bread
Salad

EQUIPMENT
Sharp knife
Chopping board
Frying-pan
Set of measuring spoons

METHOD
Thaw the prawns. If you are in a hurry run cold water over them.
Shake them dry.
    Cut the lemon into quarters. Peel and slice the garlic.
    Put the oil in the frying-pan and cook the garlic for 2 minutes.
Add the prawns. Stir and cook for a couple of minutes.
    Serve with bread and salad.

TIPS
Prepared garlic is sold in tubes and jars. Just read the tube or jar
for the suggested equivalent amount. It keeps for six weeks in the
fridge.

POACHED SALMON

Serves 1   ⏱ *Preparation 3 min, Cooking 20 min – Easy*

INGREDIENTS
1 salmon steak or cutlet, about 200 g or 8 oz
1 tablespoon oil
$^1\!/_2$ glass of any dry wine
Few sprigs of dill

EQUIPMENT
Baking dish
Set of measuring spoons
Aluminium foil

METHOD
Put the salmon steak in the baking dish. Pour the oil on the top.
Add the wine (or a couple of tablespoons of water). Put the dill on
top. Cover the dish with foil. Put into a preheated oven at 180°C,
350°F, Gas mark 4 for 20 minutes.

ADDITIONS & ALTERNATIVES
Serve with salad or new potatoes.

   You can cook this in a saucepan over a low heat. Just add a bit
more liquid and make sure the saucepan lid fits. Simmer very
gently and don't let it boil dry.

BAKED TROUT

Serves 1   ⓘ *Preparation 5 min, Cooking 20 min – Easy*

INGREDIENTS
1 medium trout, gutted and descaled
1 lemon
1 pack fresh dill, or 1 teaspoon dried dill
Salt and freshly ground pepper to taste
1 tablespoon butter

EQUIPMENT
Sharp knife
Chopping board
Set of measuring spoons
Ovenproof dish
Aluminium foil

METHOD
Wash the trout thoroughly. Cut the lemon into slices. Wash and drain two sprigs of dill. Open up the fish and put all the dill and half the lemon slices and butter inside. Add some salt and pepper.

Put the remaining slices of lemon and the butter on the outside of the fish. Wrap in aluminium foil. Put in an ovenproof dish. Cook in the oven at 180°C, 350°F, Gas mark 4 for 20 minutes.

ADDITIONS & ALTERNATIVES
Serve with boiled new potatoes and vegetables or green salad or potato salad.

Substitute orange, grapefruit or lime slices for the lemon.

SALMON IN PASTRY

Serves 2–4   ⏲ *Preparation 5 min, Cooking 20 min – Easy*

INGREDIENTS
375 g pack pre-rolled puff pastry
2 cups pre-cooked salmon or salmon trout or 500g (1 lb) salmon
2 tablespoons freshly chopped parsley
100 g (4 oz) button mushrooms (about 10)
1 tablespoon oil
2 tablespoons milk

EQUIPMENT
Set of measuring cups
Bowl
Sharp knife
Chopping board
Set of measuring spoons
Saucepan
Wooden spoon
Baking tray

METHOD
Thaw the pastry according to the instructions on the packet. Four hours in the fridge seems typical.

Flake the salmon. Discard the skin and bones. Wash and chop the parsley. Wipe the mushrooms clean. Discard any nasty ones. Chop the end off the stalks. Chop coarsely.

Heat the oil in the pan and add the mushrooms and the parsley. Cook for about three minutes, stirring. Add the flaked salmon. Stir and heat for a couple of minutes more. Take the pan off the heat.

Unroll the pastry, and cut in half to make two squares. Take one piece of pastry and lay flat. Put the salmon mixture in a line up the middle. Leave enough pastry at the edge to fold over the top and overlap. Use a finger to moisten the edge of the pastry with milk. Fold the pastry over the top of the salmon and pinch the edges together. You should end up with a small log shape.

Rub some butter or oil on the baking tray. Carefully put the roll on the tray with the join underneath. Brush some milk on the top. Make some small cuts in the top of the pastry.

Cook according to the instructions on the packet of pastry, about 20 to 30 minutes in a preheated oven at 200°C, 400°F, Gas mark 6.

ADDITIONS & ALTERNATIVES

If you need to cook the salmon use the Poached Salmon recipe on page 126.

Substitute a tin of salmon. Break it up and get rid of the bones and skin.

Use puff pastry and roll it yourself. There are full instructions on rolling pastry in the 'How to' chapter.

Use the rest of the pastry for Cheat's Chocolate Croissants (page 56).

SEA PIE

Serves 4 to 6 ⏱ *Preparation 10 min, Cooking 65 min – Easy*

INGREDIENTS

500 g (1 lb) old potatoes (about 6 medium)
Freshly ground pepper
1 tablespoon butter
About 6 tablespoons of milk (⅓ cup)
1 medium onion
1 cup milk for cooking the fish
500 g (1 lb) cod, haddock or hake fillet
1 tablespoon freshly chopped parsley

EQUIPMENT

Vegetable peeler
Sharp knife
Chopping board
2 saucepans
Set of measuring spoons
Potato masher
Set of measuring cups
Ovenproof dish
Fork

METHOD

Peel the potatoes, cutting away any nasty bits, and cutting out any eyes. Chop the potatoes into quarters. Boil for 25 minutes until soft. Drain. Add freshly ground pepper and 1 tablespoon butter and 2 tablespoons of milk. Mash thoroughly, making sure with the fork that there are no lumps.

Peel and chop the onion. Put the milk, fish and onion in a saucepan and heat over a moderate heat. Simmer for about 10 minutes. Take the pan off the heat.

Drain the fish and onions. Break the fish into lumps, throwing away any bones or skin, and put it in the bottom of the ovenproof dish with the onion and the parsley. Season with pepper. Spread the potato on top. Use a fork to make swirls and ridges. This increases the surface area and makes the top crisper.

Cook in a preheated oven at 200°C, 400°F, Gas mark 6 for about 30 minutes until crisp and brown.

ADDITIONS & ALTERNATIVES

Add 100 g of thawed pre-cooked pink prawns to the fish, about a cup full.

Add 2 oz grated cheese to the mashed potato.

Add a chopped hard-boiled egg to the fish.

Add 6 chopped button mushrooms to the fish.

Neil's anarchist fish pie: make the pie as above, but before putting in the oven use a teaspoon to make a circle with an 'A' in it. Fill this with tomato ketchup then cook in the oven.

TIPS

Use King Edward's or Désirée Reds potatoes and not new potatoes.

TUNA IN SAUCE

Serves 2   ① *Preparation 5 min, Cooking 25 min – Easy*

INGREDIENTS
1 sweet red pepper
3 tablespoons olive oil
3 cloves garlic
2 medium onions
1 tablespoon chilli sauce
227g small tin tomatoes
1 glass wine (optional)
2 fresh tuna steaks (not tinned)

EQUIPMENT
Sharp knife
Chopping board
Set of measuring spoons
Saucepan
Garlic crusher
Wooden spoon
Tin opener

METHOD
Wash the sweet red pepper. Chop the top off, and remove the seeds. Chop the pepper into very small cubes.

Put a tablespoon of oil in the saucepan. Peel and crush the garlic into the pan. Peel and chop the onion. Fry the onion for about three minutes till it is golden, stirring to stop it sticking. Add the sweet pepper and the chilli sauce and fry for another couple of minutes.

Open the tin of tomatoes. Pour the juice into the saucepan. Use the wooden spoon to mash the tomatoes while they are still in the can. Pour the mashed tomatoes into the pan. Continue to cook, stirring as the mixture boils. If you have wine, add a glass. Turn down the heat till the mixture is simmering. Add the tuna steaks. Cook for another 5 to 10 minutes.

ADDITIONS & ALTERNATIVES
Serve with rice or oven chips and salad, or boiled new potatoes.

Instead of the chilli sauce and the sweet pepper use red Spanish mojo, if you can find it.

Substitute half a teaspoon of chilli powder for the chilli sauce.

TIPS
Prepared garlic is sold in tubes and jars. Just read the tube or jar for the suggested equivalent amount. It keeps for six weeks in the fridge.

TUNA RICE

Serves 2   *① Preparation 5 min, Cooking 25 min – Easy*

INGREDIENTS
$1\frac{1}{2}$ cups rice
Salt
400 g tin chick peas
200 g medium tin tuna
1 small onion
1 clove garlic
2 cm (1 inch) fresh ginger
$\frac{1}{2}$ teaspoon turmeric
Soy sauce
Freshly ground black pepper

EQUIPMENT
Sharp knife
Chopping board

Frying-pan
Saucepan
Wooden spoon
Tin opener
Set of measuring spoons
Set of measuring cups

METHOD

Read the instructions on the rice packet for the cooking time (about 20 mins). Cook the rice in 3 cups of water with 1 teaspoon of salt. Bring to the boil. Give it a stir, turn the heat down and put a lid on the pan and simmer. When the rice is cooked and all the water has been absorbed, take the pan off the heat. There are full instructions on cooking rice in the 'How to' chapter.

Open and drain the tins of chick peas and tuna. Peel and chop the onion and garlic. Peel the ginger. Chop into tiny bits.

Fry the onion for a minute, stirring. Add the garlic, ginger and turmeric and cook for another couple of minutes. Take off the heat.

When the rice is cooked add it to the frying-pan with the chick peas and tuna. Stir it round. Warm through.

Serve with soy sauce and black pepper.

STUFFED PLAICE

Serves 4   ⏱ *Preparation 10 min, Cooking 20 min – Easy*

INGREDIENTS
600 g pack frozen small plaice fillets (about 5 fillets)
2 tablespoons fresh parsley
100 g (4 oz) mushrooms (about 10)
Salt and freshly ground pepper to taste
1 tablespoon butter
1 glass white wine

EQUIPMENT
Sharp knife
Chopping board
Set of measuring spoons
Ovenproof dish
Aluminium kitchen foil
Small jug

METHOD
Thaw the fish enough to be able to roll it. Wash the fish and drain. Wash, drain and chop the parsley. Wipe the mushrooms clean. Discard any nasty ones. Cut the end off the stalks. Chop the mushrooms into small bits.

Mix the mushrooms and one tablespoon of parsley together. Get a fish and put a tablespoon of mushroom and parsley in the middle. Roll up the fish, so it is like a sausage. Put the fish in the ovenproof dish. Season with salt and pepper. Put the butter on the fish in little blobs. Pour the wine into the dish. Cover the dish with aluminium foil. Cook in a preheated oven at 170°C, 325°F, Gas mark 3 for 20 minutes. Pour the juice from the ovenproof dish into a small jug and stir in the other tablespoon of parsley.

ADDITIONS & ALTERNATIVES
Serve with new potatoes, green vegetables or salad.

Add a small carton (142 ml or 5 fl oz) of single cream to the wine.

SQUID RINGS IN BATTER

Serves 2 to 4 ⏱ *Preparation 5 min, Cooking about 10 min – Easy*

INGREDIENTS
500 g (1 lb) prepared cleaned medium to large squid tubes
1 pack batter mix
Oil for frying
1 lemon

EQUIPMENT
Sharp knife
Chopping board
Bowl
Frying-pan
Kitchen paper
Slotted spoon or fish slice

METHOD
Cut the squid into rings. Make up the batter mix in the bowl according to the instructions on the packet. Put the squid rings in the batter.

Pour oil in the frying-pan to about 1 cm (half an inch) deep and put on the heat. After a couple of minutes, drip a bit of batter into the oil. If it sizzles and puffs up the oil is hot enough. If not wait.

When the oil is hot enough, put some of the rings in the oil, one at a time. Don't put too many in at a time or they will stick together. After a minute or so, depending on how hot the oil is, turn them over. They are ready when they are golden brown on both sides and the batter looks crisp. Fish the rings out and put on a plate covered in kitchen paper. It helps absorb the oil. If you have an oven you can put them in to keep warm at 140°C, 275°F, Gas mark 1. Serve with lemon.

ADDITIONS & ALTERNATIVES

Great starter for a Greek meal, or main dish with salad.

Use 1 pack of ready-battered squid rings. Read the instructions on the packet. They will probably need to be cooked for about 10 to 15 minutes in a hot oven. Put the squid rings on the baking tray. Spread them out so they don't overlap too much or the ones underneath will still be solid when those on top are crispy. Can be cooked straight from frozen.

TIPS

Cleaned and prepared squid tubes should have no skin and also had the 'quill' (a kind of clear plastic backbone) removed. Check they have before cutting into rings.

FISH STEW WITH CHICK PEAS

Serves 4   ① *Preparation 5 min, Cooking 15 min – Easy*

INGREDIENTS
3 cloves garlic
1 large onion
400 g tin chopped tomatoes
400 g tin chick peas
2 tablespoons chopped parsley
750 g (1½ lb) white fish, cod or hake
1 tablespoon oil
½ teaspoon hot chilli powder

EQUIPMENT
Sharp knife
Chopping board
Tin opener
Set of measuring spoons
Saucepan
Wooden spoon

METHOD
Peel and chop the garlic and onion. Open the tin of tomatoes. Open the tin of chick peas and drain the liquid off. Wash, drain and chop the fresh parsley. Chop the fish into 2.5 cm (1 inch) chunks.

Put the oil in a large pan. Add the onions, garlic and chilli. Fry for a couple of minutes, stirring to stop it sticking. Add the fish and fry for another couple of minutes. Add the tomatoes and cook on a low heat till the fish is almost done, about 5 to 10 minutes. Add the chick peas and cook for another five minutes. Add the parsley and serve.

138

Serve with crusty bread and salad.

Prepared garlic is sold in tubes and jars. Just read the tube or jar for the suggested equivalent amount. It keeps for six weeks in the fridge.

MEDITERRANEAN FISH

Serves 4–6   ① *Preparation 20 min, Cooking 25 min – Moderate*

INGREDIENTS
750 g (1½ lbs) potatoes (about 8 medium)
3 tablespoons oil
500 g (1 lb) white fish (hake, cod or haddock)
2 tablespoons flour
Salt and freshly ground pepper to taste
340 g tin black pitted olives
1 cup frozen peas
500 g bottle of Passata
50 g tin anchovies

EQUIPMENT
Vegetable peeler
Sharp knife
Chopping board
Saucepan
Set of measuring spoons
Large ovenproof dish (30 by 18 cm)
Plastic bag
Frying-pan
Wooden spoon
Kitchen paper roll

Tin opener
Set of measuring cups

METHOD

Peel and chop the potatoes into quarters. Boil them in the saucepan until nearly cooked (about 20 minutes), then drain.

Put a tablespoon of oil in the bottom of the ovenproof dish. Chop the potatoes into 1 cm (half-inch) thick slices. Spread them over the bottom of the dish.

Cut the fish into big bite-sized pieces. Put the flour in the plastic bag with a little salt and pepper. Put a few lumps of fish in the bag and, holding the top tightly closed, shake them up. They will get coated in flour. Pick them out. Repeat till all the fish is coated.

Heat 2 tablespoons of the oil in the frying-pan. Add some of the fish and fry for a couple of minutes on both sides. Don't put too many bits of fish in at a time or they stick together in an unappealing mass. When the fish is golden haul it out and drain on some kitchen towel.

Put the fish on top of the potatoes. Put the olives and peas on the potatoes. Pour passata over the peas and olives. Open the tin of anchovies and drain. Chop them and scatter them on top of the passata. Cook for 20 minutes in a preheated oven at 180°C, 350°F, Gas mark 4.

ADDITIONS & ALTERNATIVES

Try chopped or mashed tinned tomatoes instead of the passata.

MEAT

GAMMON & PINEAPPLE

Serves 1–4   ℗ *Preparation 2 min, Cooking 15 min – Easy*

INGREDIENTS
227 g tin pineapple slices (4 slices)
1 gammon steak per person

EQUIPMENT
Tin opener
Grill

METHOD
Open the tin of pineapple. Put the gammon on the grill pan. Cook for 5 to 10 minutes each side. Put it on a plate with a slice of pineapple on top.

ADDITIONS & ALTERNATIVES
Serve with salad and new potatoes.

Try a fresh peach or nectarine sliced up instead of the pineapple.

Eat any leftover pineapple chopped on breakfast cereal.

LAMB KEBABS

Serves 2–3   ⏲ *Preparation 10 min plus 1–2 hours to marinade,
Cooking 20 min – Easy*

INGREDIENTS
500 g (1 lb) lean lamb
2 tablespoons olive oil
2 tablespoons lemon juice
1 teaspoon dried mint
1 teaspoon salt

EQUIPMENT
Sharp knife
Chopping board
Set of measuring spoons
Bowl
Wooden spoon
4 metal skewers
Grill

METHOD
Cut the lamb into 2 cm (1 inch) cubes. Put the oil, lemon juice, mint and salt in the bowl. Add the lamb and mix round. Cover and put in the fridge. If possible leave for at least an hour and up to 12 if you like.

Thread the meat on the skewers. Grill for about 20 minutes till well cooked. Turn it from time to time.

ADDITIONS & ALTERNATIVES
Serve with rice, salad, and wedges of lemon.

Cut a sweet pepper into squares and thread these on the skewers between the meat.

Try small onions or cherry tomatoes between the meat.

This can be cooked on a barbecue.

SAUSAGES

Serves 2   ⓘ *Preparation 1 min, Cooking 15 min – Easy*

INGREDIENTS
200 g (8 oz) sausages

EQUIPMENT
Grill
Fork

METHOD
Prick the skin of the sausages. This stops them bursting. Cook slowly under a moderate grill for 10 to 15 minutes, turning frequently.

ADDITIONS & ALTERNATIVES
Serve with eggs, bacon, baked beans, fried onions, mashed potato or grilled tomato.

The more meat in the sausages the better. There are few tastier foods than a herby, meaty sausage, and few worse than bland, mass-produced extruded stodge. Buy your sausages with care and attention. Supermarkets do various qualities of sausage and butchers often make their own.

Sausage sandwiches for two
Cook the sausages. Meanwhile, butter four slices of bread. Peel and chop a large onion. Put 2 tablespoons of oil in a frying-pan and heat over a moderate heat. Fry the onion for about five minutes till it is brown stirring to stop it sticking. Take off the heat. Cut the sausages in half lengthways. Put on the bread. Add the fried onions, and tomato sauce and/or mustard to taste.

STEAK IN CREAM

Serves 2   ⏱ *Preparation 2 min, Cooking 15 min – Easy*

INGREDIENTS

200 g (8 oz) button mushrooms, about 20–30
1 tablespoon butter
Freshly ground pepper to taste
2 beef steaks (sirloin, rump or fillet)
2 tablespoons Worcestershire sauce
1 tablespoon mushroom ketchup (not essential)
1 medium carton (284 ml or 10 fl oz) of single cream

EQUIPMENT

Sharp knife
Chopping board
Set of measuring spoons
Frying-pan
Wooden spoon

METHOD

Wipe the mushrooms clean. Discard any nasty ones. Chop the end off the stalks. Slice the mushrooms.

Heat the butter in the frying-pan. Grind pepper on top of the steaks. Sprinkle with a few drops Worcestershire sauce. Put in the pan, pepper side down. Cook on hot for a minute, moving them round so they don't stick. Grind more pepper on the top. Sprinkle with a few more drops Worcestershire sauce. Turn the steaks over. Cook for another minute. Turn the heat to medium and cook for a further 3 to 10 minutes, depending on how you like them. Take the steaks out and let them stand on a warm plate.

Put the mushrooms in and stir round to absorb the juices. Add a teaspoon of butter if it gets too dry. Add the rest of the Worcestershire sauce and the mushroom ketchup. Cook for a

144

minute. Add the cream. Warm through (about 30 seconds). Pour over the steaks.

ADDITIONS & ALTERNATIVES

Serve with green salad.

Lea & Perrins make a well known Worcestershire sauce.

Mushroom ketchup is a thin brown liquid, which you may find in the supermarket.

You can grill the steaks with a little knob of butter, Worcestershire sauce and pepper.

If you bash the steak with a steak hammer or the end of a rolling pin before cooking it makes it more tender. Fillet steak will be tender anyway.

BEEF IN BEER

Serves 4 ① *Preparation 5 min, Cooking 2 hours – Easy*

INGREDIENTS
1 kg (2 lbs) beef, chuck steak or braising steak
200 g (8 oz) button mushrooms, about 20
2 large onions
2 carrots
1–2 tablespoons oil
1 bay leaf
1 tablespoon mixed herbs
2 tablespoons of tomato purée
500 ml tin brown ale
Salt and freshly ground pepper to taste

EQUIPMENT
Sharp knife
Chopping board
Frying-pan
Casserole with lid
Set of measuring spoons

METHOD
Cut the beef into 2 cm (1 inch) cubes. Wipe the mushrooms clean. Discard any nasty ones. Chop the end off the stalks. Peel the onions. Chop coarsely. Peel the carrots. Chop coarsely.

Put the oil in the frying-pan. Fry the beef chunks for about 2–3 minutes to brown. Stir. Put all the ingredients in the casserole. Stir round once. If the beer does not cover the ingredients either add more beer or a little water. Put the lid on the casserole. Cook for 2 hours at 140°C, 275°F, Gas mark 1.

Serve with potatoes or rice.

TIPS

Tomato purée comes in tubes. It keeps for four weeks in the fridge.

BRAISED BEEF

Serves 2–3   ① *Preparation 15 min, Cooking 90 min – Easy*

INGREDIENTS
2 large onions
3 large carrots
500 g (1 lb) braising beef
1 tablespoon oil
1 glass of wine (optional)
Salt and freshly ground pepper to taste
2 beef stock cubes

EQUIPMENT
Sharp knife
Chopping board
Set of measuring spoons
Casserole dish with lid
Wooden spoon

METHOD
This is best cooked slowly in the oven, but it can be made in a saucepan on the top

Peel and slice the onions. Peel and slice the carrots. Cut the beef into large pieces.

Put the oil in the casserole. Put the beef, onion and carrot in and mix it round. Add a glass of wine if available. Season with salt and pepper. Crumble the stock cubes up into the casserole and stir round. Top up with water to cover the ingredients. Give it a stir. Put the lid on the casserole. Cook in a preheated oven at 150°C, 300°F, Gas mark 2 for an hour and a half.

TIPS

This can be cooked in a saucepan for 90 minutes on a low heat. Stir from time to time and top up with fluid if it looks dry.

This is one of the tenderest ways of cooking a very cheap cut of meat.

GREEK LAMB KLEFTIKOS

Serves 6   ① *Preparation 10 min, Cooking 90 min – Easy*

INGREDIENTS
12 frozen lamb chump chops (1.5 kg or 3 lbs)
3 cloves garlic
2 tablespoons parsley
2 teaspoons dried rosemary
400 g tin tomatoes
1 stock cube
Salt and freshly ground pepper to taste

EQUIPMENT
Sharp knife
Chopping board
Casserole with lid
Wooden spoon
Tin opener
Set of measuring spoons

DEFROSTING

Make sure chops are thoroughly thawed. Thaw in a single layer for 3–4 hours at room temperature or overnight in a fridge.

METHOD

Trim off the excess fat. Put the chops in the casserole. Peel and chop the garlic. Add the garlic. Add the parsley and rosemary. Open the tin of tomatoes. Add to the casserole. Add stock cubes crumbled into 500 ml (1 pint) hot water. Season with salt and pepper. Cook in a preheated oven for two and a half hours at 150°C, 300°F, Gas mark 2.

ADDITIONS & ALTERNATIVES

Serve with rice and salad.

TIPS

Prepared garlic is sold in tubes and jars. Just read the tube or jar for the suggested equivalent amount. It keeps for six weeks in the fridge.

Packs of chump chops come from the freezer cabinet.

IRISH STEW

Serves 4   ⏲ *Preparation 10 min, Cooking 90 min – Easy*

INGREDIENTS

3 large potatoes
2 large onions
2 large carrots
2 small turnips
500 g (1 lb) lamb or beef
2 tablespoons sunflower oil
Salt
Freshly ground black pepper
1 stock cube
½ cup frozen peas
Bread

EQUIPMENT

Sharp knife
Chopping board
Vegetable peeler
Large saucepan
Set of measuring spoons
Set of measuring cups
Wooden spoon

METHOD

Peel the potatoes, cutting away any nasty bits, and cutting out any eyes. Chop the potatoes into small dice. Peel and chop the onions. Peel the carrots, cutting off both ends. Chop into small cubes. Peel the turnips. Chop into small cubes. Chop the meat into 2.5 cm (1 inch) cubes.

Put the oil in the saucepan and heat over a moderate heat. Fry the onion for about three minutes till it is golden, stirring to stop it sticking. Add the meat and cook for about 5 minutes, till it is

150

browned. Add the potatoes, carrots and turnips, salt and pepper, and cook for 5 minutes. Add stock cube and 750 ml ($1\frac{1}{2}$ pints) water. Bring to the boil, turn down the heat till it is just boiling (simmering). Put the lid on and cook for 1 hour.

Add the peas. Cook for 10 minutes.

Serve as it is with bread.

ADDITIONS & ALTERNATIVES

You can add sausages to the stew to make it go further.

PORK & CIDER

Serves 4   ① *Preparation 5 min, Cooking 2 hours – Easy*

INGREDIENTS
1 large onion
4 large pork chops, about 1 kg (2 lb) in total
1 large cooking apple
250 ml bottle of cider

EQUIPMENT
Sharp knife
Chopping board
Casserole with lid
Apple corer

METHOD
Peel and chop the onion. Put the onion in the bottom of the casserole. Put the chops on top. Peel the apple, discarding the seeds and core. Slice the apple and spread over the chops. Add the cider. Put the lid on the casserole.

Cook for two hours in a preheated oven at 150°C, 300°F, Gas mark 2.

ADDITIONS & ALTERNATIVES
Serve with rice and salad or potatoes and green vegetable.

SHEPHERD'S PIE

Serves 3–4   ⏲ *Preparation 15 min, Cooking 40 min – Easy*

INGREDIENTS

750 g (1½ lb) old potatoes (about 7 medium)
Salt and freshly ground pepper to taste
1 tablespoon butter
1 tablespoon milk
1 onion
2 carrots
1 tablespoon sunflower oil
500 g (1 lb) minced lamb or beef
1 stock cube

EQUIPMENT

Vegetable peeler
Sharp knife
Chopping board
Saucepan
Set of measuring spoons
Potato masher or fork
Grater
Frying-pan
Wooden spoon
Set of measuring cups
Ovenproof dish, at least 5 cm (2 inches) deep

METHOD

Peel the potatoes and chop in quarters. Boil in a saucepan with at least a pint of water and a teaspoon of salt for 20 to 25 minutes till soft. Drain and mash with the butter and milk. Add a quarter teaspoon of freshly ground pepper. Keep mashing the potatoes till they are smooth and lump free.

While the potatoes are cooking, peel and chop the onion. Peel and grate the carrots, cutting off the top and bottom. Put the oil in the frying-pan and fry the onions for a couple of minutes, stirring round. Add the meat and cook for another five minutes. Add the carrot, stock cube and 1 cup (280 ml or half pint) of water. Cook for another five minutes till most of the water has boiled off.

Put the meat mixture in the casserole. Level off the surface. Put the mashed potato on top. Spread to cover. Make artistic swirls, or whatever, in the mashed potato. Cook in a preheated oven at 180°C, 350°F, Gas mark 4 for 20 to 30 minutes till golden on top.

ADDITIONS & ALTERNATIVES

Sprinkle 50 g (2 oz or 1 cup) grated Cheddar cheese on the potato, or even in it while you are mashing.

Add 100 g (4 oz) chopped mushroom to the meat.

New potatoes make awful mashed potato. Only use old potatoes like King Edward's or Désirée Reds.

TOAD IN THE HOLE .

Serves 3 to 4   ① *Preparation 5 min, Cooking 35 min – Easy*

INGREDIENTS
1 packet batter mix
1½ tablespoons oil
8 chipolata sausages (225 g or 8 oz)
200 g (8 oz) pack streaky bacon (optional)

EQUIPMENT
Set of measuring spoons
Ovenproof dish
Wooden spoon
Bowl
Grill or frying-pan

METHOD
Make the batter mix according to the instructions on the packet, following directions for Yorkshire pudding.

Put the oil in the ovenproof dish and put in the oven at 200°C, 400°F, Gas mark 6.

Gently grill or fry the sausages for about 10 minutes, turning from time to time. You can wrap bacon round the sausage before cooking.

Take the dish out of the oven. Add the sausages and pour the batter mix on top. Return to the oven and cook for 20 to 25 minutes till golden. Follow the packet instructions for cooking Yorkshire pudding.

ADDITIONS & ALTERNATIVES
Serve with salad or green vegetables and apple sauce. There is a recipe for fresh apple sauce on page 162.

PORK CHOPS WITH ORANGE SAUCE

Serves 2 ⓘ *Preparation 5 min, Cooking 20 min – Easy*

INGREDIENTS
1 tablespoon oil
2 pork chops, about 500g (1 lb)
1 orange
1 teaspoon of cornflour
Salt and freshly ground pepper to taste

EQUIPMENT
Set of measuring spoons
Frying-pan
Wooden spoon
Zester
Sharp knife
Chopping board
Juicer
Teacup

METHOD
Put the oil in the frying-pan on a medium heat. Fry the pork chops. Start by sealing the chops on both sides by cooking on medium to high heat for a minute or so a side. Turn down the heat and cook on low for about 20 minutes, turning from time to time.

Meanwhile scrape the rind off the orange with the zester. Juice the orange. Put the cornflour in the cup. Dissolve the cornflour by adding a teaspoon of water at a time and stirring.

Take the pan off the heat. Take the chops out of the pan. Add the orange rind to the pan. Stir. Add the orange juice and three tablespoons of water. Add the dissolved cornflour stirring all the time. Put the pan on a low heat and stir till the sauce goes thick.

Season with salt and pepper. Put the chops back in the pan and coat the chops in sauce.

ADDITIONS & ALTERNATIVES
Serve with rice or salad.

ROAST BEEF

Serves 4 ① *Preparation 5 min, Cooking 45 mins per pound – Easy*

INGREDIENTS
6 small onions
1 to 1.5 kg (2 to 3 lb) rib of beef
Salt and freshly ground pepper to taste

EQUIPMENT
Sharp knife
Roasting tin/ovenproof dish
or
Cast-iron casserole
Set of measuring cups

METHOD
Peel the onions. Season the beef well with salt and freshly ground black pepper. If you are using a roasting dish or ovenproof dish, just put the beef in with the onions and half a cup of water. Cover the top with foil.

If you have a cast-iron casserole (le Creuset or similar) put the beef in with the onions and half a cup of water and roast with the lid on.

Cook in a pre-heated oven at 170°C, 325°F, Gas mark 3 for 100 minutes per kilo (45 minutes a pound). Take the lid off for the last half hour.

When the beef is cooked, take it out of the oven and put it on a plate. Leave it for 10 minutes before carving it.

ADDITIONS & ALTERNATIVES

Traditional accompaniments are mustard, horseradish sauce and Yorkshire pudding.

Serve with roast potatoes and vegetables or mashed potatoes. Put the prepared vegetables in an ovenproof dish with half a cup of oil or so. Cook at the top of the oven for at least an hour. Full instructions are in the vegetarian section.

TIPS

There's a recipe for Gravy on page 111, if you need it.

Yorkshire pudding often fails, either burning, failing to rise or turning out stodgy. You can buy frozen Yorkshire puddings and really they are as good as you can make. If you are feeling brave there are packets of batter mixes. Just follow the instructions.

Cornish pasty, beef and tomato sandwiches and beef in gravy are all ways of using up left-over beef.

You can shred left-over beef and add it to a Chinese stir fry.

ROAST LAMB

Serves 4
⏲ *Preparation 5 min,*
Cooking 45 mins per pound – Easy

INGREDIENTS
6 small onions
Half leg of lamb or shoulder of lamb, about 1–1.5 kg (2–3 lb)
1 tablespoon of rosemary
Salt and freshly ground pepper to taste

EQUIPMENT
Sharp knife
Roasting tin/ovenproof dish
or
Cast-iron casserole
Set of measuring spoons
Set of measuring cups

METHOD
Peel the onions. Season the lamb with salt and pepper and sprinkle with rosemary. If you are using a roasting dish or ovenproof dish, just put the lamb in with the onions and half a cup of water. Cover the top with foil.

If you have a cast-iron casserole (le Creuset or similar) put the lamb in with the onions and half a cup of water and roast with the lid on.

Cook in a preheated oven at 170°C, 325°F, Gas mark 3 for 100 minutes per kilo (45 minutes a pound). Take the lid off for the last half hour.

When the lamb is cooked, take it out of the oven and put it on a plate. Leave it for 10 minutes before trying to carve it.

ADDITIONS & ALTERNATIVES

Serve with roast potatoes and vegetables or mashed potatoes. Put the prepared vegetables in an ovenproof dish with half a cup of oil or so. Cook at the top of the oven for at least an hour. Full instructions are in the vegetarian section.

Redcurrant jelly goes well with lamb.

Garlic Roast Lamb
Peel 4 cloves of garlic and cut in half. Make 8 stabs in the meat and push a piece of garlic in each before cooking.

Mint sauce
Put 1 teaspoon of mint sauce in a small jug with a teaspoon of sugar and 2 tablespoons of white wine vinegar.

TIPS
There's a recipe for gravy on page 111, if you need it.

Cornish Pasty and Shepherd's Pie can be made with left-over lamb. Recipes are included.

Sandwiches with pickle and salad are pretty good too.

ROAST PORK

Serves 4   ⏱ *Preparation 2 min, Cooking 45 mins*
per pound – Easy

INGREDIENTS
1 to 1.5 kg (2 to 3 lb) loin of pork
Salt and freshly ground pepper to taste

EQUIPMENT
Sharp knife
Roasting tin/ovenproof dish
or
Cast-iron casserole
Set of measuring cups

METHOD
Perhaps the most important thing about roast pork is the crackling. To get good crackling, just make cuts about 2 cm (1 inch) apart through the skin. Rub salt into skin.

If possible stand the pork on a metal rack to keep it out of the juices as it cooks. You will survive without the metal rack.

If you are using a roasting dish or ovenproof dish, put the pork in with half a cup of water. Do not cover.

If you have a cast-iron casserole (le Creuset or similar) put the pork in with half a cup of water.

Cook for 90 minutes per kilo (40 minutes a pound). When the pork is cooked, take it out of the oven and put it on a plate. Leave it for 10 minutes before carving.

ADDITIONS & ALTERNATIVES
Serve with roast potatoes and vegetables or mashed potatoes. Put the prepared vegetables in an ovenproof dish with half a cup of oil or so. Cook at the top of the oven for at least an hour. Full instructions are in the vegetarian section.

A traditional accompaniment is apple sauce. It's the next recipe.

TIPS

There's a recipe for gravy on page III, if you need it.

Left-over pork can be cut into thin strips and made into a Chinese stir fry, or curried.

APPLE SAUCE

2 cups   ① *Preparation 5 min, Cooking 10 min – Easy*

INGREDIENTS

4 large cooking apples (about 750 g or 1½ lbs)
2 tablespoons of brown sugar
1 tablespoon lemon juice
½ teaspoon of mixed spice, nutmeg or allspice (optional)

EQUIPMENT

Sharp knife
Chopping board
Set of measuring spoons
Saucepan
Wooden spoon

METHOD

Peel the apples. Cut out the core and seeds and discard. Slice the apples about 1 cm (half-inch) thick. Put the apples, sugar, lemon juice and spice in the pan and mix together. Cook over a low heat for about 10 minutes, to soften it. Let it cool down and serve.

GOULASH

Serves 6   ⏱ *Preparation 10 min, Cooking 90 min – Moderate*

INGREDIENTS
1 kg (2 lb) stewing beef
1 kg (2 lb) onions (about 4 large)
3 cloves garlic
1 kg (2 lb) potatoes (about 8 medium)
3 tablespoons sunflower oil
400 g tin chopped tomatoes
2 tablespoons paprika pepper
2 stock cubes
1 medium carton (284 ml or 10 fl oz) sour cream

EQUIPMENT
Sharp knife
Chopping board
Set of measuring spoons
Large saucepan
Wooden spoon
Tin opener

METHOD
Chop the meat into 2.5 cm (1 inch) cubes. Peel and slice the onions. Peel and slice the garlic. Peel and slice the potatoes.

Heat 2 tablespoons of oil in the saucepan. Add the onion and garlic and fry for a couple of minutes, stirring to stop it sticking. Add the meat and cook and stir for about 5 minutes. Add another tablespoon of oil and the potatoes and cook for another 5 minutes.

Open the tin of tomatoes and add to the mixture. Add the paprika. Add 500 ml water (1 pint) and the stock cubes. Cook for an hour on a low heat so it is just boiling (simmering). Stir from time to time to stop it sticking. If it looks like it is drying out add more fluid. The potato and onion should go to a thick gravy.

Just before serving, add the sour cream and stir round.

ADDITIONS & ALTERNATIVES

Serve with rice, green salad and bread.

Try pork or lamb instead of the beef.

STEAK & KIDNEY

Serves 4–6   ① *Preparation 15 min, Cooking 2 hours – Moderate*

INGREDIENTS

2 tablespoons flour
Salt and freshly ground pepper to taste
1 kg (2 lb) steak and kidney
200g (8 oz) button mushrooms (about 20 to 25)
1 large onion
1 tablespoon olive oil
1 bay leaf
1 tablespoon mixed herbs
1 stock cube

EQUIPMENT

Plastic bag
Set of measuring spoons
Sharp knife
Chopping board
Frying-pan
Wooden spoon
Casserole with lid

METHOD

Put the flour and some salt and pepper in the plastic bag. Chop the meat into 2.5 cm (1 inch) cubes. Put the steak and kidney in the bag, a few chunks at a time. Hold the bag shut and shake to cover in flour.

Wipe the mushrooms clean. Discard any nasty ones. Chop the end off the stalks. Peel and chop the onion.

Put the oil in the frying-pan and heat over a moderate heat. Fry the onion for about three minutes until golden, stirring to stop it sticking. Fish the onion out of the pan and put in the casserole dish. Fry the steak and kidney for a minute or so to seal it, stirring. It does not need to be cooked through. Put the meat in the casserole with the bay leaf and herbs and mushrooms.

Stir any of the remaining flour from the bag in the frying pan for 15 seconds with a tablespoon of water. Add to the casserole. Crumble the stock cube on top. Cover the meat with water. Put a lid on the casserole. Cook for 2 hours at 150°C, 300°F, Gas mark 2.

ADDITIONS & ALTERNATIVES

Serve with potatoes and vegetables.

You can use a glass of wine instead of some of the water.

TIPS

If you are using a cast-iron casserole, you can fry the onions and meat in it and dispense with the frying-pan.

STUFFED BREAST OF LAMB

Serves 2–3   ① *Preparation 5 min, Cooking 45 min*
                                         – Moderate, messy

INGREDIENTS
1 boned breast of lamb about 500 g (1 lb)
170 g pack of stuffing mix

EQUIPMENT
Sharp knife
Chopping board
String or 2 metal skewers
Ovenproof dish

METHOD
Get the butcher to take the bones out of the breast of lamb. This is a fatty cut and benefits from having the stuffing mixture.

Lay down the breast of lamb skin side out. Cut five lengths of string longer than the breast of lamb and lay them under the breast of lamb. If you are using metal skewers forget this instruction.

Mix up the stuffing according to the instructions on the packet. This generally involves adding boiling water, stirring round and leaving to stand. Spoon the stuffing on to the breast of lamb along a line 5 cm (2 inches) from the shorter edge. Starting from this edge, roll the breast of lamb into a sausage. Secure it. Tie the strings round the breast of lamb or stick the metal skewers through to the middle.

Put the breast of lamb on the ovenproof dish. Cook in a preheated oven at 170°C, 325°F, Gas mark 3 for 45 minutes. Slice to serve.

ADDITIONS & ALTERNATIVES
This can be eaten hot with potatoes and vegetables, or cold with pickle and salad.

MINCE ROLL

Serves 3–4 ○ *Preparation 15 min, Cooking 30 min – Moderate*

INGREDIENTS

375 g pack pre-rolled puff pastry (chilled or frozen)
1 large onion
2 cloves garlic
2 slices of bread or 1–2 cups breadcrumbs
500 g (1 lb) mince
2 tablespoons freshly chopped parsley
Salt and freshly ground pepper to taste
1 egg

EQUIPMENT

Sharp knife
Chopping board
Baking tray
Wooden spoon
Bowl
Set of measuring spoons
Set of measuring cups

METHOD

Thaw the pastry according to the instructions on the packet. Four hours in the fridge seems typical.

Peel and chop the onion. Peel and chop the garlic. Crumble the bread into crumbs with your fingers.

Put the mince, onion, garlic, breadcrumbs, parsley, salt and pepper in the bowl. Break the egg into a cup. Fish out any bits of shell. Add the egg to the bowl. Mix it all together.

Open the pastry and spread it out flat. It should be oblong. The intention is to get the meat mixture on the pastry and seal it in to make a fat sausage shape. The pastry will stick together if it is moistened with some water or milk. If you don't seal it like this it will all fall apart. If it is too difficult to roll one large mince roll, cut the pastry in half and make two small ones.

Start from a short edge of the pastry. Put the meat mixture on the pastry in a thick sausage shape, leaving a gap at the edge. Pull the pastry over the top so it overlaps. Moisten the edges and gently press them together. Seal up the ends of the sausage shape by using water and pressing the pastry together.

Get the baking tray and rub with a little oil. Put the roll on the baking tray, turning it over as you do, so the join is on the bottom. Brush a little milk on top to give it a shine when it is cooked. Stab a few holes with a fork so the steam can get out as it cooks.

Cook in a pre-heated oven at 200°C, 400°F, Gas mark 6 for 30 minutes.

Slice and serve hot with vegetables or cold with salad.

ADDITIONS & ALTERNATIVES
Add 2 tablespoons mixed herbs.

There may be enough pastry left over to make a sweet mince pie roll (same principle, different filling) or jam roll (spread jam thickly on pastry leaving 2.5 cm (1 inch) margin, then roll like a Swiss roll).

TIPS
Prepared garlic is sold in tubes and jars. Just read the tube or jar for the suggested equivalent amount. It keeps for six weeks in the fridge.

CORNISH PASTY

Makes 2   ① *Preparation 10 min, Cooking 25 min*
If you ever cook roast beef, this is an easy way of using
up the remains

INGREDIENTS
375 g pack of pre-rolled puff pastry or shortcrust pastry
1 cup left-over beef
1 cup left-over potatoes
$\frac{1}{2}$ cup chopped carrot
Salt and freshly ground pepper to taste
1 teaspoon of milk

EQUIPMENT
Sharp knife
Chopping board
Set of measuring cups
Wooden spoon
Bowl
Baking sheet
Set of measuring spoons

METHOD
Thaw frozen pastry according to the instructions on the packet. Four hours in the fridge seems typical.

Unfold the pastry. Cut the pastry into 15 cm (6 inch) squares.

Chop up the meat, potato and carrots and mix together in the bowl with some salt and pepper. Put a couple of tablespoons of mixture in the middle of each pastry square. Moisten the edge of the pastry and pull the edges together over the top like a crest. Pinch together. Use a fork to make a couple of holes. Lay on a baking sheet. Brush the pastry with a little milk to gloss it up.

Cook in a preheated oven at 190°C, 375°F, Gas mark 3 for 20 to 25 minutes till golden brown.

ADDITIONS & ALTERNATIVES

You can use lamb, peas, or any cooked vegetables for the filling.

Use a block of prepared pastry and roll it yourself. Full instructions are in the 'How to' chapter.

GRILLED STEAK

Serves 1 ⏲ *Preparation 3 min, Cooking 15 min – Moderate*

INGREDIENTS
150–200 g (6–8 oz) fillet, rump, or sirloin steak cut
   2.5 cm (1 inch) thick
1 tablespoon olive oil
Freshly ground pepper

EQUIPMENT
Sharp knife
Chopping board
Grill
Set of measuring spoons

METHOD
Cut through the fat every inch or so. If the meat is very lean, brush a tablespoon of olive oil on it. Season with fresh ground pepper.

Turn the grill on full and let it get really hot. Put the steak on the grill pan. Cook for one minute each side. Turn down the grill to medium and cook for 10 to 15 minutes depending on thickness. Turn the steak over every two minutes or so. This should give a medium done steak with a pink inside.

If you like your steak rare, cook for a shorter time, if you like it well done then give it longer. Also if it is a thinner cut it will take less time.

This is one recipe where practice and experience helps. If you want a reasonably foolproof right-first-time steak recipe try the Steak in Cream on page 144.

ADDITIONS & ALTERNATIVES

Serve with chips, salad, grilled tomato, fried onions or fried mushrooms.

Add a few drops of Worcestershire sauce to the steak during cooking.

Marinade for 24 hours in 3 tablespoons of soy sauce and 1 tablespoon of oil in a fridge.

TIPS

If you bash the steak with a steak hammer or the end of a rolling pin before cooking it makes it more tender. Fillet steak will be tender anyway.

BEEF STEW WITH WINE

Serves 4–6 ① *Preparation 10 min, Cooking 2 hours – Moderate*
You have to keep adding things as it cooks

INGREDIENTS
1.5 kg (3 lbs) beef, chuck steak or braising steak
2 tablespoons flour
Salt and freshly ground pepper to taste
200 g (8 oz) button mushrooms (20 to 25)
200 g (8 oz) belly pork
12 small onions
1 tablespoon olive oil
1 bay leaf
1 teaspoon marjoram or oregano
1 bottle red wine
1 tablespoon parsley

EQUIPMENT
Sharp knife
Chopping board
Plastic bag
Set of measuring spoons
Frying-pan
Wooden spoon
Bowl
Casserole with lid

METHOD
Cut the beef into 2.5 cm (1 inch) cubes. Put the flour and some salt and pepper in the plastic bag. Put the beef in the bag, a few chunks at a time. Hold the bag shut and shake to cover in flour.

Wipe the mushrooms clean. Discard any nasty ones. Chop the end off the stalks. Cut the belly pork into thin slices then chop small. Peel the onions. Keep whole. Do not slice.

Put the oil in the frying-pan and heat over a moderate heat. Fry the mushrooms for a minute or so, stirring till they are coated. Lift the mushrooms out and put in the bowl.

Fry the belly pork and onions for about three minutes, stirring to stop it sticking. Lift out the pork and onions and put in the bowl.

Fry the beef chunks for a few minutes in the oil left from the belly pork to seal it. Put the beef in the casserole with the bay leaf and oregano. Cover the meat with a half and half mixture of wine and water. Cook for an hour at 150°C, 300°F, Gas mark 2.

Add the mushrooms, onions and pork. Cook for another hour. Add the parsley when ready to serve.

ADDITIONS & ALTERNATIVES

Serve with potatoes or rice.

Belly pork is what streaky bacon is made from and should have a lot of fat. If you can't find it try four rashers of bacon, chopped.

Try marinating the meat in the wine overnight in the fridge.

The better the wine, the better the dish tastes.

You can use just a glass of wine, using water and a stock cube to make up the rest of the fluid.

VEGETARIAN

MASHED POTATO

Serves 3–4   ⏱ *Preparation 5 min, Cooking 25 min – Easy*

INGREDIENTS

750 g (1½ lb) old potatoes (about 7 medium)
1 tablespoon butter
Salt and freshly ground pepper to taste

EQUIPMENT

Sharp knife
Chopping board
Saucepan
Potato masher
Set of measuring spoons

METHOD

Peel potatoes and chop in quarters. Put in a saucepan and cover with water. Add a teaspoon of salt and boil for 20 to 25 minutes till soft. Drain and mash with the butter. Add a quarter teaspoon of fresh ground pepper. Keep mashing the potatoes till they are smooth and lump free. If you want them creamier add a little more butter or a splash of milk.

ADDITIONS & ALTERNATIVES

Sprinkle 50 g (2 oz or 1 cup) grated Cheddar cheese on the potato, or even in it while you are mashing.

TIPS

New potatoes make awful mashed potato. Only use old potatoes like King Edward's or Désirée Reds.

VEGETARIAN SAUSAGE & FRIED ONIONS

Serves 2   ⓘ *Preparation 5 min, Cooking 10 min – Easy*

INGREDIENTS

2 large onions
1 tablespoon olive oil
250 g pack of vegetarian sausages

EQUIPMENT

Sharp knife
Chopping board
Frying-pan
Set of measuring spoons
Grill

METHOD

Peel and chop the onion. Put the oil in the frying-pan and heat over a moderate heat. Fry the onion for about 8 to 10 minutes till it is well cooked, stirring to stop it sticking.

Grill the sausages for about 10 minutes, turning them from time to time.

ADDITIONS & ALTERNATIVES

Eat with mashed potato and apple sauce or in a bread roll.

BAKED POTATO & FILLINGS

Serves 1 ⏱ *Preparation 5 min, Cooking 60 min – Easy*

INGREDIENTS
1 large potato
1 tablespoon butter
Salt and freshly ground pepper to taste

EQUIPMENT
Fork
Skewer
Aluminium foil
Oven glove
Set of measuring spoons

METHOD
Wash the potato. Prick the surface with a fork. Stick the skewer through the potato, it helps it to cook in the middle. Wrap the potato in aluminum foil.

Cook in a preheated oven on the top shelf at 230°C, 450°F, Gas mark 8 for an hour. It is ready when it gives when pressed. Remember to use oven gloves!

If you like your potato crisp on the outside, cook it for half an hour with the foil on, then take it off and cook for another half an hour.

Take out the skewer. Split the potato. Add butter, salt and pepper to taste with one of the suggested fillings:
Half a cup of grated Cheddar cheese
1 small tin baked beans
Left over (or a tin of) chilli con carne
1 small carton of sour cream and chopped fresh chives
Tuna mayonnaise (see p. 30)

ROAST POTATOES, CARROTS, PARSNIP & ONION

Serves 2 or vegetable for 4   ⏲ *Preparation 10 min,*
                                          Cooking 40 min – Easy

INGREDIENTS
6 medium or 3 large potatoes
4 medium carrots
2 parsnips
8 small onions
2 tablespoons sunflower oil

EQUIPMENT
Sharp knife
Chopping board
Ovenproof dish
Vegetable peeler
Set of measuring spoons

METHOD
Peel the potatoes, cutting away any nasty bits, and cutting out any eyes. Chop the potatoes in half if medium sized or into quarters if large.

Peel the carrots, cutting off both ends. Chop the carrots lengthways into quarters. Peel the parsnips, cutting off both ends. Chop the parsnips lengthways into quarters. Peel the onions.

Put the potatoes, onions, carrots and parsnips in the ovenproof dish with the oil. Cook in the top of a preheated oven at 180°C, 350°F, Gas mark 4 for 40 to 60 minutes or longer if you like them really well done.

Turn over half-way through cooking.

TIPS

Heat the oil first by putting the dish with the oil in the oven for about 10 minutes before adding the vegetables. It helps to reduce sticking. You can cook this with any roast meat. If you are cooking the meat at a lower temperature just cook the vegetables for longer.

STUFFED TOMATO

Serves 4   ① *Preparation 5 min, Cooking 10 min – Easy*

INGREDIENTS
8 button mushrooms
$\frac{1}{2}$ tablespoon parsley
1 medium onion
$\frac{1}{2}$ tablespoon butter
4 large beef tomatoes
2 tablespoons grated cheese
1 egg
Salt and freshly ground pepper

EQUIPMENT
Sharp knife
Chopping board
Set of measuring spoons
Saucepan
Wooden spoon
Baking sheet

METHOD

Wipe the mushrooms clean. Discard any nasty ones. Cut the end of the stalks. Chop the mushrooms.

Wash, drain, dry and finely chop the parsley. Peel and chop the onion.

Put the butter in the saucepan and heat over a moderate heat. Fry the onion for about two minutes, stirring to stop it sticking. Take the pan off the heat.

Cut a 'lid' off the stalk end of the tomatoes. Scoop out the pulp from the tomato and add to the pan. Cook on a low heat for about three minutes. Take the pan off the heat. Add the mushrooms, parsley, cheese and egg. Mix together. Add salt and pepper to taste. Fill the tomato shells.

Put on the baking sheet and cook in a preheated oven at 200°C, 400°F, Gas mark 6 for 5 minutes.

BUTTER BEANS & TOMATO

Serves 2   ① *Preparation 2 min, Cooking 10 min – Very Easy*

INGREDIENTS
2 cloves garlic
1 medium onion
1 tablespoon olive oil
140 g small tin tomato purée
1 teaspoon mixed herbs
1 vegetable stock cube
400 g tin butter beans

EQUIPMENT
Garlic crusher
Sharp knife
Chopping board
Set of measuring spoons
Saucepan
Wooden spoon
Set of measuring cups
Tin opener

METHOD

Peel and crush the garlic into the pan. Peel and chop the onion.

Put the oil in the pan and heat over a moderate heat. Fry the onion and garlic for about three minutes until golden, stirring to stop them sticking. Add the tomato purée, herbs and stock cube. Stir. Add half a cup of water. Heat up and stir.

Open the tin of butter beans and drain off the fluid. Add the butterbeans to the pan. Heat up for about three minutes.

ADDITIONS & ALTERNATIVES

Serve with rice and salad.

Try other beans like haricot.

Sprinkle the top with grated cheese.

Use half a tube of tomato purée instead of the tin.

TIPS

Prepared garlic is sold in tubes and jars. Just read the tube or jar for the suggested equivalent amount. It keeps for six weeks in the fridge.

AUBERGINE, CHICK PEA & TOMATO STEW

Serves 4   ⏲ *Preparation 10 min, Cooking 50 min – Easy*

INGREDIENTS
2 large aubergines about 700 g ($1\frac{1}{2}$ lb)
2 onions
2 tablespoons of oil for frying
2 cloves garlic
1 teaspoon turmeric
$\frac{1}{2}$ teaspoon chilli powder
400 g tin tomatoes
2 x 400 g tins chick peas
Juice of 1 lemon
1 tablespoon parsley or coriander leaf
Pitta bread

EQUIPMENT
Sharp knife
Chopping board
Big pan or a wok
Set of measuring spoons
Garlic crusher
Wooden spoon
Tin opener
Cup

METHOD
Wash the aubergines and cut into slices, discarding the top and bottom. Soak the slices in water for a few minutes, then drain.

Peel and chop the onions. Put the oil in the pan. Peel and crush the garlic into the pan. Add the onion and cook on a medium heat for 5 minutes. Stir from time to time. Add the turmeric and chilli

181

powder. Cook for another three minutes.

Add the aubergine slices and stir round until they start to cook and are golden, about ten minutes. Add the tin of tomatoes, mashing up if required.

Open the tins of chick peas. Pour the liquid off into a cup, you may need it later. Add the chick peas to the mixture. Stir it all together and cook on a medium heat (don't burn it) for about 35 minutes. If it starts to get too dry looking, add the chick pea liquid. If this runs out use water.

Just before serving, put in the lemon juice and parsley or coriander.

Serve with warm pitta bread (sprinkle them with water and grill for a minute, till they puff up).

ADDITIONS & ALTERNATIVES

Try eating this with Tabbouleh (page 83), an appropriate salad.

TIPS

Dutch Aubergines don't need soaking.

Prepared garlic is sold in tubes and jars. Just read the tube or jar for the suggested equivalent amount. It keeps for six weeks in the fridge.

WHITE SAUCE

Makes about 500 ml (1 pint)

*① Preparation 2 min,
Cooking 5 min – Easy*

INGREDIENTS
4 tablespoons butter
6 tablespoons flour
500 ml (1 pt or 2 cups) milk
Salt and freshly ground pepper to taste

EQUIPMENT
Set of measuring spoons
Saucepan
Wooden spoon

METHOD
The secret of this sauce is to keep stirring.

Put the butter in the pan. Melt over moderate heat. Mix in the flour, and cook for a minute, stirring all the time. Take off the heat. Add the milk a bit at a time. Stir each time to make sure it is smooth. When all the milk is added put it back on the heat and bring to the boil. Keep stirring. Reduce the heat and simmer gently for 2 minutes, stirring. Season with salt and pepper.

TIPS
This is quite a thick sauce. If you want it thinner, just add a little more liquid.

CHEESE SAUCE

Makes about 500 ml (1 pint)　　　　　　① *Preparation 2 min,*
　　　　　　　　　　　　　　　　　　　　　Cooking 5 min – Easy

INGREDIENTS
2 tablespoons butter
2 tablespoons flour
500 ml (1 pt or 2 cups) milk
75 g (3 oz) mature Cheddar cheese (grated), about 1½ cups
Salt and freshly ground pepper to taste

EQUIPMENT
Saucepan
Wooden spoon
Grater for the cheese
Set of measuring spoons
Set of measuring cups

METHOD
The secret of this sauce is to keep stirring.

Put the butter in the pan. Melt over moderate heat. Mix in the flour and cook for a minute, stirring all the time. Take off the heat. Add the milk a bit at a time. Stir each time to make sure it is smooth. When all the milk is added put it back on the heat and bring it to the boil. Keep stirring. Reduce the heat and simmer gently for 2 minutes, stirring. Take off the heat.

Grate the cheese. Add the cheese to the sauce and mix. Continue to stir till the cheese has melted into the sauce. Season with salt and pepper.

ADDITIONS & ALTERNATIVES
Try other cheeses.

Add a teaspoon of whole grain mustard.

Use ready grated cheese.

184

CAULIFLOWER CHEESE

Serves 4   ① *Preparation 10 min, Cooking 30 min – Easy* ·

INGREDIENTS
500 ml (1 pint) cheese sauce (previous recipe)
100 g (4 oz) mature Cheddar cheese, about 2 cups
1 medium cauliflower

EQUIPMENT
Grater for the cheese
Sharp knife
Chopping board
Saucepan
Wooden spoon
Ovenproof dish

METHOD
Make the cheese sauce. Add the extra cheese.

Break up the cauliflower. Throw away the leaves. Wash the cauliflower. Put the cauliflower in the pan with 2 cm (1 inch) water. Boil gently for 7 minutes. Drain and put into the ovenproof dish. Pour the cheese sauce over the cauliflower.

Cook in a preheated oven at 180°C, 350°F, Gas mark 4 for 15 minutes till golden brown.

ADDITIONS & ALTERNATIVES
Serve with boiled new potatoes.

Add grilled bacon or fake bacon (e.g. Protoveg 'Sizzles' or Betty Crocker 'Bac-Os').

COURGETTE & TOMATO BAKE

Serves 2   ① *Preparation 5 min, Cooking 20 min – Easy*

INGREDIENTS

3 large tomatoes (about 500 g or 1 lb)
6 courgettes (about 500 g or 1 lb)
2 tablespoons olive oil
1 tablespoon fresh basil or a teaspoon of dried
2 tablespoons fresh breadcrumbs
3 tablespoons grated Parmesan or Pecorino cheese
Freshly ground pepper

EQUIPMENT

Sharp knife
Chopping board
Set of measuring spoons
Frying-pan
Wooden spoon
Bowl
Casserole

METHOD

Wash and slice the tomatoes. Wash, trim and drain the courgettes. Cut the courgettes lengthways into 1 cm (half inch) slices.

Fry the slices of courgette in the oil over a medium heat until slightly softened. Cook enough at a time to cover the bottom of the pan. Scatter some of the basil on the courgettes.

Put a layer of courgettes in the bottom of the casserole. Add a layer of sliced tomato. Alternate layers of courgette and tomato.

Mix the breadcrumbs and cheese in the bowl. Spread the breadcrumbs and cheese over the top. Season with pepper.

Cook in a preheated oven at 200°C, 400°F, Gas mark 6 for 10 to 15 minutes till the top is browned.

POTATO PIE

Serves 4   ① *Preparation 5 min, Cooking 45 min – Easy*

INGREDIENTS

1 kg (2 lbs) potatoes (about 8 medium)
1 egg
300 ml ($\frac{1}{2}$ pint) milk, about $1\frac{1}{4}$ cups
$\frac{1}{4}$ teaspoon ground nutmeg
Salt and freshly ground pepper to taste
1 tablespoon butter
1 tablespoon parsley

EQUIPMENT

Sharp knife
Chopping board
Bowl
Set of measuring cups
Ovenproof dish
Set of measuring spoons

METHOD

Peel the potatoes, cutting away any nasty bits, and cutting out any eyes. Cut into small pieces.

Break the egg into the bowl. Fish out any bits of shell. Add the milk, nutmeg, salt and pepper. Mix with a fork.

Arrange the bits of potato in the ovenproof dish. Pour the milk mix over the potatoes. Put little knobs of butter on top. Cook in a preheated oven at 200°C, 400°F, Gas mark 6 for about 45 minutes.

Take it out of the oven. Scatter the parsley on the top.

ADDITIONS & ALTERNATIVES

Serve with green salad.

Add grated cheese as you serve it.

MEATLESS CHILLI

Serves 2–3   ① *Preparation 10 min, Cooking 20 min – Easy*

INGREDIENTS
150 g packet dried soya mince, Protoveg Burgamix or
    350 g pack Quorn mince
100 g (4 oz) or about 10 mushrooms (optional)
1 large onion
2 tablespoons oil
1 packet Mexican chilli seasoning
400 g tin tomatoes
400 g tin red kidney beans
1 cup rice
Salt to taste

EQUIPMENT
Bowl
Sharp knife
Chopping board
Set of measuring spoons
Frying-pan
Wooden spoon
Tin opener
Saucepan
Set of measuring cups

METHOD
Soak the soya mince in water according to instructions. This takes about 10 minutes. Or follow the instructions for the Burgamix.

If using mushrooms, wipe the dirt off and cut the end off the stalk. Slice roughly. Peel and chop the onion.

Put the oil in the frying-pan. Fry the onion over a medium heat for a couple of minutes to soften, stirring to stop it sticking. Add the Mexican chilli seasoning and salt and mix well.

Open the tin of tomatoes. Pour in the juice from the tin and then mash up the tomatoes in the tin with a wooden spoon. Add the mashed up tomatoes. Stir and bring to the boil. Turn down the heat so the mixture is just boiling.

Drain the mince and add to the pan. Open the tin of kidney beans and drain off the liquid. Add the beans to the pan. Add the mushrooms. Stir from time to time. If it looks like it is getting too dry then add some water. Cook for 5 minutes. Take off the heat.

You can let it cool and reheat when the rice is done. It seems that the flavour improves with reheating.

Serve with boiled rice, American long grain being the best for this. Look at the packet to see how long to cook it. There are full instructions on boiled rice in the 'How to' chapter.

ADDITIONS & ALTERNATIVES

Read what it says on the packet of seasoning to get the right amount. Try substituting half to one teaspoon chilli powder and 2 teaspoons ground cumin for the seasoning mix.

Try adding a small tin of sweet corn.

Add 1 chopped sweet pepper.

For 4–6 people double up the quantities.

VEGETARIAN SHEPHERD'S PIE

Serves 3–4   ⏱ *Preparation 10 min, Cooking 30 min – Easy*

INGREDIENTS

150 g packet dried soya mince, or Protoveg Burgamix
750 g (1½ lb) old potatoes (about 7 medium)
Salt and freshly ground pepper to taste
1 tablespoon butter
1 tablespoon milk
1 onion
2 carrots
1 tablespoon sunflower oil
1 vegetable stock cube
2 teaspoons Marmite or yeast extract

EQUIPMENT

Bowl
Vegetable peeler
Sharp knife
Chopping board
Saucepan
Set of measuring spoons
Potato masher
Grater
Frying-pan
Wooden spoon
Set of measuring cups
Ovenproof baking dish, at least 5 cm (2 inches) deep

METHOD

Soak the soya mince for about 10 minutes while the potatoes are cooking, or follow the instructions for the Burgamix.

Peel the potatoes. Chop into quarters. Put them in a saucepan and cover with water. Add a teaspoon of salt and boil for 20 to 25 minutes till soft. Drain and mash the potatoes with the butter and milk. Add a quarter teaspoon of freshly ground pepper. Keep mashing the potatoes till they are smooth and lump free.

Meanwhile, peel and chop the onion. Peel and grate the carrots, cutting off the top and bottom. Put the oil in the frying-pan and fry the onions for a couple of minutes, stirring round.

Drain the soya mince. Add it, or the Protoveg mix, the carrot, stock cube, Marmite and 1 cup of water to the pan. Cook for another five minutes till most of the water has boiled off.

Put the meat mixture in the casserole. Level off the surface. Put the mashed potato on top. Spread to cover. Make artistic swirls or whatever in the mashed potato.

Cook in a preheated oven at 180°C, 350°F, Gas mark 4 for 15 to 20 minutes till golden on top.

ADDITIONS & ALTERNATIVES

Use broken up vegetarian hamburger instead of the soya mince. Sprinkle 1 cup (50 g or 2 oz) grated Cheddar cheese on the potato, or even in it while you are mashing.

Add 100 g (4 oz or about 10) chopped mushrooms to the meat substitute.

New potatoes make awful mashed potato. Only use old potatoes like King Edward's or Désirée Reds.

VEGETABLE LASAGNE

Serves 6   ① *Preparation 15 min, Cooking 60 min – Moderate*

INGREDIENTS

1 quantity of *Vegetarian Bolognese sauce*
3 cloves garlic
2 onions
1 tablespoon olive oil
400 g tin Italian plum tomatoes
2 teaspoons oregano, mixed herbs or mixed Mediterranean herbs
500 g (1 lb) minced Quorn or other mince substitute
Salt and freshly ground pepper to taste
White Sauce
4 tablespoons butter
6 tablespoons flour
2 cups milk (500 ml or 1 pint)
1–2 tablespoons grated Parmesan cheese
Salt and freshly ground pepper to taste

250 g packet of lasagne pasta (look for 'No pre-cooking required' on the packet)
1 tablespoon grated Parmesan cheese

EQUIPMENT

Garlic crusher
Sharp knife
Chopping board
Set of measuring spoons
Frying-pan
Tin opener
Wooden spoon
Saucepan
Set of measuring cups
Flat ovenproof dish (2 litre or $3\frac{1}{2}$ pints)

METHOD

To make the Vegetarian Bolognese sauce

Peel and crush the garlic. Peel and chop the onion. Put the oil in the frying-pan and warm over a medium heat. Fry the garlic and chopped onion on a medium heat for about two minutes. Stir them every half a minute or so.

Open the tin of tomatoes. Pour the juice into the frying-pan. Use the wooden spoon to mash the tomatoes while they are still in the can (it's easier than chasing them round the pan). Pour the mashed tomatoes into the pan. Continue to cook, stirring as the mixture boils. Add your chosen herb. Cook for another five minutes or so until the fluid has reduced and the sauce is less sloppy.

The sauce can be improved by adding a glass of wine and cooking a bit longer. Take off the heat. Add the Quorn mince and stir. Season with salt and pepper.

To make the white sauce

Melt the butter in a saucepan over a low heat. Add flour and stir together to make a smooth paste. Take the pan off the heat. Continue to stir and add the milk a bit at a time. If you add it too quickly it will go lumpy. When all the milk has been added, put it back on the heat and add one or two tablespoons of Parmesan cheese. Stir until it thickens. Season with salt and pepper. Take off the heat.

Assemble the lasagne in the ovenproof dish. Start with a layer of Bolognese sauce. Cover with a layer of lasagne pasta. Then a layer of Bolognese sauce. Next a layer of white sauce. Then pasta, Bolognese, white sauce.

However many layers you do it must end up with white sauce on top. Sprinkle the top with Parmesan cheese. Cook in a preheated oven at 180°C, 350°F, Gas mark 4 for about 30 minutes. The top should be brown.

DESERTS

BANANA CUSTARD

Serves 2   ① *Preparation 2 min, Cooking 3 min – Easy*

INGREDIENTS
2 ripe bananas
350 ml tub of Fresh Custard

EQUIPMENT
Sharp knife
Chopping board
Saucepan
Wooden spoon

METHOD
Peel the bananas and chop into slices. Put the custard in the pan
and warm, stirring. When the custard is warm add the banana and
stir round. Serve.

ADDITIONS & ALTERNATIVES
'Fresh Custard' can be found in the chiller cabinet at the
supermarket.

Use other ready-made custards in cartons or tins.

MARINADED ORANGES

Serves 2, easy to double up ① *Preparation 10 min; needs to stand for at least 2 hours – Easy*

INGREDIENTS
2 large oranges
2 tablespoons of Cointreau
1 tablespoon of sugar
1 small carton (142 ml or 5 fl oz) single cream or
    natural unsweetened yoghurt

EQUIPMENT
Sharp knife
Chopping board
Bowl
Set of measuring spoons

METHOD
Peel the oranges and cut off the pith (the bitter white stuff under the skin). Cut into 1 cm (half-inch) slices. Try and dig out the pips. Put the orange slices in the bowl with the Cointreau and the sugar. Put in the fridge for at least two hours.

Arrange artistically on a plate and serve with the cream or yoghurt.

ADDITIONS & ALTERNATIVES
Try rum or brandy instead of the Cointreau.

BANANA SPLIT

Serves 2   ① *Preparation 5 min – Easy*

INGREDIENTS
2 bananas
1 tub vanilla ice-cream or other favourite flavour
Squirty raspberry sauce (comes in a plastic bottle)
Squirty cream (comes in a spray can)
2 cocktail cherries
Hundreds and thousands (from the baking section)

EQUIPMENT
Sharp knife
Chopping board
2 bowls

METHOD
Peel the bananas. Cut in half lengthways. Lay out in the bowls. Put a couple of scoops of ice-cream between the bananas. Put some raspberry sauce on top of the ice-cream. Do a couple of lines of squirty cream down the sides. Sprinkle the top with some hundreds and thousands. Serve with a cherry on top.

ADDITIONS & ALTERNATIVES
Use different sauces like strawberry or chocolate.
   Garnish with a sprig of mint.

ICE CREAM SUNDAES

Serves as far as it will go ① *Preparation 5 min – Easy*

INGREDIENTS
A matter of choice
At least 2 kinds of ice cream, preferably of different colours
   (vanilla, strawberry, pistachio, coffee)
Squirty sauces (raspberry, chocolate, butterscotch)
Glacé cherry
Chopped nuts

EQUIPMENT
Tall glasses
Long spoons

METHOD
It is a truth universally acknowledged that a restaurant in need of
a profit sells ice cream.

Assemble the ingredients of your choice, topping it off with
sauce, cream and chopped nuts and a glacé cherry.

Hire someone in braces and a striped shirt to sing as it comes
in.

Forget the sparklers.

ADDITIONS & ALTERNATIVES
Make it in bowls.

Put chopped fresh fruit in and go easy on the sauces.

TIPS
A magnificent stand-by dish if your latest creation fails.

FRUIT FOOLS

Serves 2 to 4 ⓘ *Preparation 2 min, Cooling 1 hour or more – Easy*

INGREDIENTS
300 g tin raspberries
1 medium carton (284 ml or 10 fl oz) double cream

EQUIPMENT
Tin opener
Bowl
Whisk or fork

METHOD
Open tin of raspberries and drain juice into a cup. Mash up fruit.
Pour the cream into the bowl. Whisk up or beat with a fork till it
goes stiff. Mix in the mashed raspberries. Spoon into glasses or
serving bowls. Keep in the fridge for at least an hour.

ADDITIONS & ALTERNATIVES
You can use almost any tinned fruit, just drain and lightly mash.
Fresh raspberries, strawberries, blackcurrants lightly mashed.

BAKED BANANAS

Serves 4   ⏱ *Preparation 10 min, Cooking 20 min – Easy*

INGREDIENTS
4 bananas
2 or 3 tablespoons of honey
2 tablespoons rum
2 tablespoons brown sugar
2 tablespoons water

EQUIPMENT
Sharp knife
Chopping board
Set of measuring spoons
Teacup
Baking dish

METHOD
Peel the bananas. Chop in half lengthways. Mix the honey, rum, water and sugar in a teacup. Coat the bananas in the mixture. Bake in a preheated oven at 170°C, 325°F, Gas mark 3 for about 20 minutes.

BAKED APPLES

Serves 1   ⏲ *Preparation 5 min, cooking 20–25 min – Easy*

INGREDIENTS
1 large baking apple
$\frac{1}{2}$ tablespoon sugar
1 tablespoon raisins
$\frac{1}{4}$ teaspoon mixed spice
1 teaspoon butter

EQUIPMENT
Apple corer
Bowl
Ovenproof dish
Set of measuring spoons

METHOD
Take the core out of the apple with the corer. Mix the sugar, raisins, mixed spice and butter in the bowl. Push the mixture into the hole left by the core. Put the apple in the ovenproof dish. Pour in a couple of tablespoons of water. Cook in a preheated oven at 170°C, 325°F, Gas mark 3 for 20 to 25 minutes.

ADDITIONS & ALTERNATIVES
Serve with custard, cream or yoghurt.

Try bought mincemeat (for mince pies) instead of the sugar and raisins.

RICH CHOCOLATE POT

Serves 4

⏲ *Preparation 2 min,
Cooking 7 min – Easy*

INGREDIENTS
200 g dark chocolate
1 medium carton (284 ml or 10 fl oz) single cream
1 egg
1 drop vanilla essence
Pinch of salt

EQUIPMENT
Bowl
Saucepan
Wooden spoon
Fork

METHOD
Break the chocolate into pieces and put into the bowl. Warm the cream to boiling point. Pour over the chocolate and leave for 5 minutes for the chocolate to melt.

Add the egg, vanilla and salt. Mix with a fork until smooth. Pour into serving cups, ramekins or glasses. Cool in a refrigerator for three or four hours.

ADDITIONS & ALTERNATIVES
Serve with lightly whipped cream if required.

Put a teaspoon of Cointreau and some flaked chocolate on top.

FRUIT CRÊPES

Make one or two per person ☻ *Preparation 3 min, Cooking 10 min if you want them warm – Easy*

INGREDIENTS
1 packet ready made crêpes
500 g jar fruit compôte
    or a 400 g tin or jar of fruit pie filling
1 tablespoon butter
1 tablespoon sugar
Small carton (142 ml or 5 fl oz) of single cream

EQUIPMENT
Tin opener
Ovenproof dish (if you want them warmed)
Set of measuring spoons

METHOD
Put a couple of spoons of fruit filling on each crêpe. Roll it up. This can be eaten cold, with a little cream.

To warm up: put the rolled up crêpes in an ovenproof dish. Put a couple of dabs of butter on each crêpe and sprinkle with sugar. Warm in the oven for 10 minutes at 150°C, 300°F, Gas mark 2.

ADDITIONS & ALTERNATIVES
Use a tin of fruit instead of the compôte. Open the tin, Drain off the fluid. Mash the fruit a bit then spoon on to the crêpes.

Use fresh fruit. Try a peach sliced and then left to stand with a tablespoon of brandy or rum and a tablespoon of sugar. When you serve the crêpe pour the juice over the top.

Use natural unsweetened Greek yoghurt or vanilla ice-cream instead of the cream.

APPLE CRUMBLE

Serves 4   ⏱ *Preparation 12 min, Cooking 35 min – Easy*

INGREDIENTS
700 g (1½ lbs) cooking apples, about 3
2 tablespoons brown sugar
1 teaspoon mixed spice

For the crumble
6 tablespoons flour
3 tablespoons butter
3 tablespoons brown sugar

EQUIPMENT
Apple peeler and corer
Sharp knife
Chopping board
Saucepan
Wooden spoon
Ovenproof dish. Should be at least 5 cm (2 inches) deep
Bowl
Set of measuring spoons

METHOD
Peel, core and chop the apples. Put them in the pan with the sugar, spice and about 3 tablespoons of water. Cook over a low heat for about 10 minutes, stirring. Allow to cool down and put in ovenproof dish.

Rub the flour and butter together in a bowl with your fingertips till it makes crumbs. Stir in the sugar. Spread on the top.

Cook in a preheated oven at 200°C, 400°F, Gas mark 6 for 25 minutes.

ADDITIONS & ALTERNATIVES

Serve with yoghurt or ice-cream.

Use tinned cherry pie filling instead of the apple or substitute rhubarb.

APPLE FRITTERS

Serves 4   ① *Preparation 10 min, Cooking 10 min – Moderate*

INGREDIENTS

1 pack batter mixture
2 big cooking apples or 4 Granny Smiths
Sunflower oil for frying
1 tablespoon sugar to sprinkle on top (optional)
Lemon (optional)

EQUIPMENT

Bowl
Wooden spoon
Apple peeler and corer
Sharp knife
Chopping board
Frying-pan
Slotted spoon for fishing the fritters out of the oil
Kitchen roll
Set of measuring spoons

METHOD

Mix the batter in the bowl according to the instructions on the packet. Peel and core the apples, then slice into circles. If you don't have the corer tool then peel and cut the apple in half, cut out the core, and cut into segments. Put all the apple slices in the batter mix.

Pour oil in the frying-pan to about 1 cm (half-inch) deep and put on the heat. After a couple of minutes, drip a bit of batter into the oil. If it sizzles and puffs up the oil is hot enough. If not wait. When the oil is hot enough, put some of the rings in the oil, one at a time. Don't put too many in at a time or they will stick together. After a minute or so, depending on how hot the oil is, turn them over. They are ready when they are golden brown on both sides and the batter looks crisp.

Fish the fritters out with the slotted spoon and put on a plate covered in kitchen paper. It helps absorb the oil. If you have an oven you can put them in it to keep warm at 140°C, 275°F, Gas mark 1.

Serve them on a plate with sugar and a slice of lemon to squeeze on top.

ADDITIONS & ALTERNATIVES
Use bananas instead of apples.

CRÈME FRAÎCHE BRÛLÉE

Serves 2 to 4 ⏲ *Preparation 5 min, Cooking 5 min – Easy*

INGREDIENTS

Some fruit, e.g. grapes, raspberries, strawberries, peach slices, nectarine slices, apple slices
400 ml tub of crème fraîche
2 tablespoons brown sugar

EQUIPMENT

Sharp knife
Chopping board
2 ramekins (small ovenproof bowls) or 1 small ovenproof dish
Set of measuring spoons
Fork
Grill

METHOD

Prepare the fruit (wash, peel, slice as appropriate). Put the fruit in the bottom of the ramekins or ovenproof dish. There should be enough to half fill them.

Whip the crème fraîche with a fork till it is smooth. Put the crème fraîche on the fruit and smooth the top. Put them in the fridge till ready to serve. Then sprinkle the top with a layer of sugar up to half a centimetre (quarter inch) thick.

Heat the grill. Toast them until the sugar bubbles. Allow to cool slightly and serve.

ADDITIONS & ALTERNATIVES

Pour a teaspoon of brandy or kirsch on the fruit.

Use whipped double cream instead of the crème fraîche.

QUICK CRÈME BRÛLÉE

Serves 2   ① *Preparation 2 min, Cooking 3 min*
— *A cheat classic*

INGREDIENTS
100 g (4 oz) fruit e.g. raspberries, strawberries or blueberries
350 ml tub fresh custard
4 tablespoons brown sugar

EQUIPMENT
Sharp knife
Chopping board
2 ramekins (small ovenproof bowls) or 1 small ovenproof dish
Set of measuring spoons
Grill

METHOD
Prepare the fruit (wash, peel, slice as appropriate). Put the fruit in the bottom of the ramekins. There should be enough to make a layer. Cover with the custard and flatten. Leave enough room to put the sugar on later. Put the ramekins in the fridge till ready to serve.

Sprinkle the top with a layer of sugar up to half a centimetre (quarter inch) thick. Heat the grill. Toast the ramekins until the sugar bubbles.

Allow to cool slightly and serve.

ADDITIONS & ALTERNATIVES
'Fresh Custard' can be found in the chiller cabinet at the supermarket.

Use other ready made custard
Pour a teaspoon of brandy or kirsch on the fruit.

SHERRY TRIFLE

Serves 6   ⏱ *Preparation 5 min, Cooking 5 min*
                              – The ideal party food for children

INGREDIENTS
150 g packet sponge fingers
200 g tin mixed fruit
2 tablespoons sweet sherry
135 g packet jelly
350 ml pot Fresh Custard
1 can squirty cream
Hundreds and thousands or chocolate vermicelli
    (cake decoration)

EQUIPMENT
Bowl
Tin opener
Set of measuring spoons
Cup
Saucepan
Wooden spoon

METHOD
Get a bowl and put a layer of sponge fingers at the bottom. Open the tin of mixed fruit. Put the sherry in a cup together with a tablespoon of the syrup from the tinned fruit. Pour over the sponge fingers.

Read the instructions on the jelly packet. It probably says use half the jelly with about 300 ml (half pint or $1\frac{1}{4}$ cups) boiling water. Cut up the jelly into pieces. Put them in the boiling water and stir till they dissolve. Add the drained mixed fruit. Pour on to the sponges and leave to set, about half an hour.

Open the pot of custard. Pour on to the jelly. Keep in the fridge.

Before serving squirt a layer of squirty cream on the top. Scatter 'hundreds and thousands' on the cream.

TIPS

This is about the only use for sweet sherry except for soaking fruit.

Fresh fruit is better though more work.

RICE PUDDING

Serves 4   ① *Preparation 2 min, Cooking 120 min – Easy*

INGREDIENTS
3 tablespoons pudding rice
500 ml (1 pint or 2 cups) milk
1 tablespoon sugar
1 tablespoon butter
$\frac{1}{2}$ teaspoon ground nutmeg

EQUIPMENT
Ovenproof dish
Set of measuring spoons

METHOD
Wash the rice. Put the rice, milk and sugar in the ovenproof dish. Break up the butter into little blobs and drop them on top. Sprinkle the nutmeg on the top.

Cook in a preheated oven at 150°C, 300°F, Gas mark 2 for two hours.

TIPS

This method gives great skin.

The creamiest rice comes from cooking at 140°C, 275°F, Gas mark 1 for two and a half hours and stirring it a couple of times during cooking.

CHEAT'S APPLE STRUDEL

Serves 4   ⓘ *Preparation 15 min, Cooking 30 min – Moderate*

INGREDIENTS

2 cooking apples or 4 eating apples
$\frac{1}{2}$ cup raisins
Juice and rind of unwaxed lemon
1 tablespoon sugar
$\frac{1}{2}$ teaspoon cinnamon
1 tablespoon butter
375 g pack frozen puff pastry
$\frac{1}{2}$ cup milk

EQUIPMENT

Sharp knife
Chopping board
Vegetable peeler (optional)
Zester (optional)
Set of measuring spoons
Bowl
Set of measuring cups
Wooden spoon
Baking tray

METHOD

Thaw the pastry according to the instructions on the packet. Four hours in the fridge seems typical.

Peel the apples. Take out the core and pips. Slice it up. Put the apple into the bowl with the raisins, lemon, sugar and cinnamon.

Wipe the baking tray with a little butter or sunflower oil to stop the strudel sticking. Open the pack of pre-rolled puff pastry. Unfold it and put it on the baking tray. Spoon the apple mixture in a line up the middle of the pastry. Put little dots of butter on top of the mixture. Fold the edges of the pastry over the top. Use a little of the milk to wet the edges to help it stick together. Cut three or four slits through the top of the pastry. If you get to the mixture, stop. Brush some of the milk on the top. Sprinkle a teaspoon of sugar on top.

Cook in a preheated oven at 180°C, 350°F, Gas mark 4 for about half an hour. When it is cooked it will be golden brown.

ADDITIONS & ALTERNATIVES

Try adding sultanas or candied peel.

Get a rolling pin and roll your own bought puff pastry. There are full instructions on rolling pastry in the 'How to' chapter.

TIPS

On lemon peel. A lot of fruit has been 'treated' with various things including wax to make it shiny. It is better to look out for lemons which are marked as 'unwaxed' or even 'organic'. Leave out the lemon peel if you like.

APPLE PIE

Serves 6   ℗ *Preparation 10 min, Cooking 30 min – Easy*

INGREDIENTS
Butter for greasing
450 g pack ready rolled shortcrust pastry
4 large cooking apples (about 750 g or 1½ lbs)
2 tablespoons brown sugar
1 tablespoon lemon juice
½ teaspoon of 'apple pie spice', nutmeg or mixed spice (optional)
milk for glazing

EQUIPMENT
Pie dish
Sharp knife
Chopping board
Set of measuring spoons
Saucepan
Wooden spoon
Fork

METHOD
Rub the inside of the pie dish with a little butter or margarine.

If the pastry is frozen make sure it is thawed properly (read the instructions on the packet). Unfold the pastry. Lay the pastry over the pie dish and push it gently into place. Check there is enough pastry for the lid. Leave a margin of 2 cm (1 inch) above the lip of the dish.

Peel the apples. Cut out the core and seeds and discard. Slice the apples about 1 cm (half inch) thick. Put the apples, sugar, lemon juice and spice in the pan and mix together. Cook over a low heat for about 10 minutes, to soften it up a bit. Let it cool down a bit.

Pour the mixture into the pastry case and even out with the spoon. Wipe round the edge with a little water. Put the pastry lid on top and push the edges down to seal them. Prick some holes in the lid with a fork. Brush the top with a little milk, which makes it shiny. Cook in a preheated oven at 200°C, 400°F, Gas mark 6 for 20 to 25 minutes. The pastry will have gone golden.

ADDITIONS & ALTERNATIVES

Serve with custard, cream, ice-cream or yoghurt.

Use a block of prepared pastry and roll it yourself. There are full instructions on rolling pastry in the 'How to' chapter.

Try different fillings like apple and blackberry, or even canned pie filling.

LEMON PIE

Serves 6   ① *Preparation 15 min, Cooking 45 min*
Cooking the pastry in two stages is a bit of a fiddle,
but otherwise no problem

INGREDIENTS

450 g pack frozen shortcrust pastry
Butter for greasing
2 lemons
4 tablespoons sugar
2 eggs
200 g (8 oz) Mascarpone cheese

EQUIPMENT

Round ovenproof dish about 20–25 cm (8–10 inch) across and
    about 1 to 2 cm ($\frac{1}{2}$ to 1 inch) deep
Fork
Greaseproof paper
1 pack of dried beans to hold the pastry down
Grater
Sharp knife
Chopping board
Juicer
Bowl
Set of measuring spoons
Wooden spoon

METHOD

Make sure the pastry is thawed, about four hours in the fridge.
Unroll the pastry.

Grease the dish and then put the pastry in the dish. Pastry is
fairly flexible so you can push it into place. If it tears patch it with
a spare bit, moistening with a bit of water to make sure it sticks.

214

Pastry shrinks when it cooks so trim it above the top of the rim. Prick the bottom of the pastry with a fork at least five times to let steam out.

Cut a piece of greaseproof paper and press gently on to the pastry. Fill the bottom with a layer of cheap dried beans, for instance butter beans.

Cook the pastry case at 200°C, 400°F, Gas mark 6 for 15 minutes until the top edges go golden. Take the pastry case out of the oven.

Meanwhile make the filling. Grate the skin off the lemons and put in the bowl. Squeeze the juice into the bowl. Fish out any stray pips and discard. Add the sugar and eggs. Beat together. Add the Mascarpone and beat some more. It will take a couple of minutes to get the Mascarpone incorporated and the mixture smooth.

Take the beans and the greaseproof paper out of the pastry case. Put the lemon filling in. Cook in a preheated oven at 150°C, 300°F, Gas mark 2 for about 35 minutes till puffed up gently and brown on the top.

ADDITIONS & ALTERNATIVES

Serve on its own or with a dollop of natural set yoghurt.

Substitute 3 limes or 2 oranges for the 2 lemons.

MINCE TART

Serves 6   ① *Preparation 10 min, Cooking 30 min – Moderate*

INGREDIENTS

450 g pack pre-rolled shortcrust pastry (frozen or chilled)
Butter for greasing
450 g jar mincemeat

EQUIPMENT

Round ovenproof dish about 25 cm (10 inch) across and about 1 to
2 cm ($\frac{1}{2}$ to 1 inch) deep.

Sharp knife

METHOD

Thaw the pastry. Rub a bit of butter or margarine on the inside of
the dish. Line the dish with pastry. Cut around the edge, trimming
the extra pastry off. Don't cut it too close to the edge, cut it a bit
big because the pastry will shrink.

Fill the pie with the mincemeat. Cook in an oven at 180°C,
350°F, Gas mark 4 for about 30 minutes.

Take it out and cool. It is better not to eat it hot as the
mincemeat retains heat. Cut into slices.

ADDITIONS & ALTERNATIVES

Serve with yogurt, custard or cream.

As an option, get the rest of the pastry and lay it out flat on the
board. Cut into 1 cm (half inch) strips. Lay some of these across the
top, weaving them over and under.

Make small tarts.

Make turnovers with puff pastry. Cut circles round a saucer, put
on a tablespoon of mincemeat and fold over the edge, sealing with
a little water. Pierce with a fork to let out any steam.

Make a roll. Use pre-rolled puff pastry. Spread it with the
mincemeat and roll up. Cook and slice.

TIPS

Jars of mincemeat vary a lot in price. The cheapest are mainly
sugar. Improve the taste with alcohol and extra dried fruit.

Ready made custard is as good as that made from powder, it
just costs more.

TREACLE TART

Serves 6   ⏲ *Preparation 10 min, Cooking 30 min – Moderate*

INGREDIENTS

450 g pack frozen pre-rolled shortcrust pastry
Rind of a lemon
100 g (4 oz) breadcrumbs (this is about 4 slices of wholemeal
    bread)
6 tablespoons golden syrup
2 tablespoons treacle

EQUIPMENT

Round ovenproof dish about 25 cm (10 inch) across and about 1 to
    2 cm ($\frac{1}{2}$ to 1 inch) deep.
Grater or zester for the lemon
Set of measuring spoons

METHOD

Thaw the pastry according to the instructions on the packet,
probably about four hours in the fridge. Line the flan dish with the
pastry.

Take the zest off the lemon with the grater or zester. Mix the
breadcrumbs with the golden syrup, treacle and lemon zest.

Pour the mixture into the pastry and cook in a preheated oven
at 200°C, 400°F, Gas mark 6 for 30 minutes or so until golden.

Allow to cool before trying to get it out of the dish.

ADDITIONS & ALTERNATIVES

Serve with cream, yoghurt or ice-cream
    Try all golden syrup.

MILLE FEUILLE

Serves 6   ① *Preparation 15 min, cooking 10 to 15 min*
– Moderate

INGREDIENTS
375 g pack ready rolled puff pastry
3 tablespoons raspberry jam or other favourite jam
Squirty cream in a can
Icing sugar

EQUIPMENT
Sharp knife
Chopping board
Baking tray
Set of measuring spoons
Wire cooling rack

METHOD
Thaw the pastry according to the instructions on the packet, probably about four hours in the fridge. Open the pack of puff pastry and unfold. Cut into three equal pieces. Put the puff pastry on the baking tray and bake in a preheated oven at 200°C, 400°F, Gas mark 6 for 10 to 15 minutes, until it has puffed and gone golden. Put the puff pastry on the cooling rack and leave for at least 20 minutes.

Put the bottom layer of pastry on a plate. Spread half the jam on it and then squirt a layer of cream. Put jam on the next piece of puff pastry. Put the piece of puff pastry on the first layer. Squirt cream on the jam layer. Put the last piece of puff pastry on top. Sprinkle icing sugar on the top.

The final mille feuille should be from the bottom up, pastry, jam, cream, pastry, jam, cream, pastry and icing sugar.

ADDITIONS & ALTERNATIVES

Try putting a layer of some soft fruit like strawberries, black-berries, blueberries between the jam and the cream layer.

Try thick custard instead of the cream. Tinned or carton will not do. Make up powdered instant custard according to the instructions on the packet, but increase the amount of powder by half, so if it says use two tablespoons, use three. Let the custard cool down and go fairly solid, then spread on the jam.

Use double cream instead of squirty cream. Beat a medium carton (284 ml or 10 fl oz) of double cream with a fork or whisk till it goes stiff then spread it.

BREAD PUDDING

Serves at least 4 ⏱ *Preparation 5 min but needs to be left overnight, Cooking 90 min – Moderate*

INGREDIENTS
Half a large loaf of bread (can be stale but NOT mouldy!)
1 egg
1 cup dried fruit, sultanas, raisins, etc.
3 tablespoons brown sugar
2 tablespoons butter
1 teaspoon nutmeg

EQUIPMENT
Bowl
Wooden spoon
Ovenproof dish about 5 cm (2 inches) deep
Set of measuring spoons
Set of measuring cups

METHOD
Break up the bread, put it in the bowl, cover with water and leave it overnight or at least 2 hours. Squeeze out the water and put the bread in clean bowl.

Wipe the inside of the ovenproof dish with a little butter.

Mix the egg up in a cup. Add the egg, dried fruit, sugar, butter broken into little blobs and nutmeg to the squeezed out bread. Mix together. Put into the ovenproof dish, press down the mixture with the back of a spoon and sprinkle a little sugar on top.

Put into the oven at 150°C, 300°F, Gas mark 2 for 90 minutes. When you think it is cooked, stick a knife or skewer in. If it comes out clean it is cooked. If it comes out sticky, it needs more cooking. Take out of the oven, cut into squares whilst still in tin and allow to cool. You can eat it hot with custard if you like.

BREAD & BUTTER PUDDING

Serves 4, depending on amount ⏲ *Preparation 10 min,*
Cooking 60 min – Moderate

INGREDIENTS
Half to a whole loaf of bread (can be stale but NOT mouldy)
Butter
1 cup of dried fruit (sultanas, raisins, etc.)
4 tablespoons of sugar
2 eggs
4 tablespoons milk

EQUIPMENT
Ovenproof dish. Should be at least 5 cm (2 inches) deep
Set of measuring spoons
Set of measuring cups

METHOD
Slice the bread. Butter each slice. Wipe butter on the inside of the dish. Put in a layer of bread. Sprinkle with dried fruit and sugar. Put another layer of bread, then fruit and sugar. Finish up with a layer of bread.

Mix the eggs with the milk and pour over the top. Sprinkle with a final bit of sugar.

Put in the oven 170°C, 325°F, Gas mark 3 for an hour. Check it is cooked by sticking a knife in. If it comes out clean, it is cooked.

ADDITIONS & ALTERNATIVES
This can be eaten hot or cold, with or without custard.

Use mincemeat instead of the fruit and sugar mix.

STIR FRY PORK WITH BLACK BEAN SAUCE

Serves 4   ① *Preparation 5 min, Cooking 5 min – Easy*

INGREDIENTS
500 g (1 lb) pork fillet
1 bunch spring onions
227 g tin bamboo shoots
2 tablespoons oil
150 g jar Chinese black bean sauce

EQUIPMENT
Sharp knife
Chopping board
Tin opener
Set of measuring spoons
Wok or big frying-pan
Wooden spoon

METHOD
Cut the pork fillet into very thin slices. Clean and prepare the spring onions. Cut the root end off, trim the leaves. Peel off and discard any dried up or slimy ones. Cut into 1 cm (half inch) pieces. Open the tin of bamboo shoots and drain.

Heat the oil in the wok. Stir fry the pork till cooked, about three minutes. Add the spring onions and stir fry for another minute. Add the bamboo shoots. Add the jar of black bean sauce. Heat up and stir (about a minute).

ADDITIONS & ALTERNATIVES

Serve with rice or noodles.

Thin sliced beef can be substituted for the pork.

STIR FRY VEGETABLES

Serves 3–4   ① *Preparation 10 min, Cooking 5 min – Easy*

INGREDIENTS

1 bunch spring onions
1 red sweet pepper
100 g (4 oz) mange tout
1 pack 250 g bean sprouts
1 clove garlic
2 tablespoons oil
1 teaspoon ground five spice powder (optional)
2 tablespoons soy sauce
1 tablespoon sherry (optional)
Rice or noodles

EQUIPMENT

Sharp knife
Chopping board
Garlic crusher
Set of measuring spoons
Wok or big frying-pan
Wooden spatula

METHOD

The vegetables should be hot on the outside but still retain their crispness. Prepare everything before hand.

Clean the spring onions, chopping the root end off, trimming the leaves and throwing away any slimy bits. Wash, shake dry and shred. Wash the sweet pepper. Cut out the seeds and the stalk end. Slice the sweet pepper. Wash the mange tout peas. Wash and drain the bean sprouts. Peel the garlic.

Put the oil in the wok or deep frying-pan. Put the pan on a moderate heat. Crush the garlic into the hot oil. Add the five spice powder if you have any. Stir round. Add the spring onion, sweet pepper and mange tout. Stir and fry for about 30 seconds. Keep it all moving so that everything gets coated in oil. Add the bean sprouts. Stir for 10 seconds. Add the soy sauce and sherry. Stir fry for a couple of minutes.

Serve with boiled rice or noodles.

ADDITIONS & ALTERNATIVES
In general, broccoli, cauliflower, baby sweet corn and carrots need to be cooked for about 3 minutes. Everything else takes about 2 minutes.

All of the following are particularly suitable
100 g (4 oz) mushrooms (button, oyster, or shitake)
1 carrot peeled and cut into matchsticks
1 broccoli head
1 pack baby sweet corn
5 chopped lettuce or cabbage leaves
227 g tin water chestnut
227 g tin bamboo shoots

TIPS
Supermarkets and health food shops sell ready to cook bean sprouts.

If you are having rice or noodles, read the packet for the cooking time. Rice will take much longer to cook than the stir fry, so put it on when you have the rest of the ingredients together, but before you start cooking.

This is the quickest Chinese dish. It is very flexible. You can use almost any vegetable that you happen to have around. The secret is to prepare all the vegetables beforehand. Put them on side plates or bowls so they can go in the wok in order.

SWEET & SOUR SAUCE

Add to stir-fry   ① *Preparation 1 min, Cooking 5 min – Easy*

INGREDIENTS

1 ½ tablespoons cornflour
2 tablespoons water
5 tablespoons orange juice
3 tablespoons vinegar
2 tablespoons soy sauce
2 tablespoons sherry
1 tablespoon tomato purée
1 tablespoon sugar

EQUIPMENT

Set of measuring spoons
Cup
Saucepan
Wooden spoon

METHOD

Mix the cornflour with the water in a cup. It will form a smooth paste if you add the water a bit at a time.

Put all the other ingredients in a small pan. Heat gently. Add the cornflour mix. Heat, stirring all the time, to stop it sticking and going lumpy. As it heats up it will thicken. Take off the heat.

ADDITIONS & ALTERNATIVES

You can adjust this to your taste with more vinegar for the sour taste, or sugar for the sweet.

Substitute lemon juice for some of the orange

TIPS

This sauce can be made in quantity and frozen.

226

SWEET & SOUR CHICKEN

Serves 3–4   ⓘ *Preparation 2 min, Cooking 5 min – Easy*

INGREDIENTS
500 g (1 lb) chicken off the bone
2 tablespoons oil
1 quantity of sweet and sour sauce (previous recipe)
   or a jar of sweet and sour sauce (about 200 g)

EQUIPMENT
Sharp knife
Chopping board
Wok or frying-pan
Set of measuring spoons
Wooden spoon

METHOD
Cut the chicken into thin slices. Put the oil in the pan. Heat up. Add the chicken and stir fry until the chicken is cooked (about three to five minutes). Add the sweet and sour sauce. Stir for another minute.

ADDITIONS & ALTERNATIVES
Serve with noodles.
   Add half a sliced sweet red pepper with the seeds thrown away.
   Add a packet of bean shoots (250 g).
   Add a small tin of pineapple chunks, drained.
   Try thin sliced pork fillet instead of chicken.
   Try prawns instead of chicken.

TERIYAKI BEEF

Serves 3   ⏱ *Preparation 10 min, Cooking 7 min – Easy*

INGREDIENTS
1 bunch spring onions
500 g (1 lb) lean frying steak
227 g (8 oz) tin water chestnuts
2 tablespoons sunflower or groundnut oil
150 g jar Teriyaki sauce

EQUIPMENT
Sharp knife
Chopping board
Tin opener
Set of measuring spoons
Frying-pan or wok
Wooden spoon

METHOD
If you are having rice or noodles, read the packet for the cooking time. Rice will take longer to cook than the stir fry.

Clean and prepare the spring onions. Cut the root end off, trim the leaves. Peel off and discard any dried up or slimy leaves. Chop into thin slices.

Cut the beef into thin strips. Open the tin of water chestnuts and drain off the fluid.

Heat the oil in the frying-pan. Fry the beef, stirring all the time. It will be cooked in about 3–5 minutes. Add the spring onions and water chestnuts. Stir fry for a minute or so. Add the Teriyaki Sauce. Stir and heat.

ADDITIONS & ALTERNATIVES
Serve with rice or noodles.

TIPS

There are full instructions on cooking rice and noodles in the 'How to' chapter. Teriyaki is Japanese, but the technique is similar to Chinese.

CHINESE PORK & GINGER

Serves 4 ① *Preparation 10 min, Cooking 6 min – Moderate*

INGREDIENTS
500 g (1 lb) pork fillet
3 cloves garlic
1 cm ($\frac{1}{2}$ inch) root ginger or $\frac{1}{2}$ teaspoon dried ginger
4 spring onions
2 tablespoons oil
1 teaspoon Chinese five spice powder
2 tablespoons soy sauce

EQUIPMENT
Sharp knife
Chopping board
Set of measuring spoons
Frying-pan or wok
Wooden spoon

METHOD
Prepare everything beforehand. There is just not time while it is cooking.

Trim any fat off the pork and cut into thin strips. Peel and crush the garlic. Peel the ginger and cut into small cubes. Clean and prepare the spring onions. Cut the root end off, trim the leaves. Peel off and discard any dried up or slimy leaves. Chop into thin slices.

Put the oil in the frying-pan or wok. Heat up. Stir fry the garlic and ginger for 2 minutes. Add the pork and five spice powder and stir fry for a couple of minutes. Add the soy sauce. Heat for two more minutes.

ADDITIONS & ALTERNATIVES
Serve with rice or noodles.

TIPS
There are full instructions on cooking rice and noodles in the 'How to' chapter. You can buy prepared chopped ginger root in jars. It will keep for six weeks in the fridge.

LEMON CHICKEN

Serves 4   ⏱ *Preparation 15 min, Cooking 10 min – Moderate*

INGREDIENTS
4 chicken quarters
1 teaspoon salt
4 tablespoons sunflower or groundnut oil
1 cm ($\frac{1}{2}$ inch) root ginger or $\frac{1}{2}$ teaspoon dried ginger
4 spring onions
1 red pepper
100 g pack Chinese shitake or oyster mushrooms
1 lemon
1 teaspoon cornflour
1 tablespoon soy sauce
2 tablespoons dry sherry
1 teaspoon sugar

EQUIPMENT
Sharp knife
Chopping board
Zester
Juicer
2 cups and some plates or bowls for putting ingredients in
Frying-pan or wok
Set of measuring spoons
Wooden spoon

METHOD
Prepare everything beforehand. There is just not time while it is
cooking.

Take the chicken off the bone and cut into bite-sized chunks. Mix the pieces in the bowl with the salt and 2 tablespoons of oil.

Peel the ginger and cut into small cubes. Clean and prepare the spring onions. Cut the root end off, trim the leaves. Peel off and discard any dried up or slimy leaves. Chop into thin slices.

Wash the red pepper. Cut out the seeds and discard. Cut into thin slices. Cut the mushrooms into thin slices. Take the peel off the lemon with the zester or grate it off. If you have neither zester nor grater, peel finely with a sharp knife. Cut the peel into fine strips. Make sure you don't get any pith. Extract the lemon juice and put it in a cup. Mix the cornflour with about a tablespoon of water in a cup.

Put 2 tablespoons of oil in the frying-pan or wok. Heat up. Stir fry the chicken for five minutes. Take the chicken out of the pan. Add another tablespoon of oil to the pan if needed. Stir fry the ginger, spring onions, red pepper, mushrooms and lemon peel for 2 minutes. Add the soy sauce, sherry and sugar. Stir and add the cornflour mixture. Keep stirring as it thickens. Put the chicken back in the pan and cook for a minute. Add the lemon juice and serve.

ADDITIONS & ALTERNATIVES

Use the equivalent amount of other chicken pieces off the bone. Serve with rice or noodles. There are full instructions on cooking rice and noodles in the 'How to' chapter.

TIPS

Now you have made this any stir fry will seem simple. You can buy prepared chopped ginger root in jars. It will keep for six weeks in the fridge.

SATAY CHICKEN

Serves 2   ① *Preparation 60 min, Cooking 15 min – Easy*

INGREDIENTS
1 medium onion
2 cloves garlic
2 chicken breasts
1 tablespoon lemon juice
1 tablespoon sunflower oil
2 tablespoons soy sauce
1 teaspoon ginger powder (optional)
$\frac{1}{2}$ teaspoon cumin powder (optional)
1 tablespoon sesame oil (optional)
190 g jar satay sauce (peanut and chilli)

EQUIPMENT
Sharp knife
Chopping board
Bowl
Set of measuring spoons
Bamboo skewers
Saucepan
Wooden spoon
Grill

METHOD
Peel and chop the onion finely. Peel and chop the garlic. Cut the chicken into bite-sized chunks. Put in the bowl with the lemon juice, sunflower oil, soy sauce, ginger, cumin and sesame oil. Mix round so the chicken is coated. Leave for at least an hour to soak into the chicken.

Soak the bamboo skewers in cold water.

Make the satay sauce according to the instructions on the jar.

233

Thread the chicken pieces on to the skewers. Grill for 10 to 15 minutes, turning to make sure they are cooked on all sides.

ADDITIONS & ALTERNATIVES

Serve with rice and chopped cucumber.

Some shops sell satay marinade. Just follow the instructions.

TIPS

Satay sauce is only spiced up peanut butter. Get half a jar of unsweetened crunchy peanut butter, a cup of water, 2 tablespoons coconut powder, 2 tablespoons of soy sauce, half a teaspoon of chilli powder. Heat it in a small saucepan and stir. Cook for about five minutes.

THAI CHICKEN CURRY

Serves 2   ① *Preparation 10 min, Cooking 15–20 min – Easy*

INGREDIENTS

3 cloves of garlic
4 medium/large chicken thighs (boneless)
$2\frac{1}{2}$ cm (1 inch) root ginger or 1 teaspoon powdered ginger
1 lime
2 tablespoons sunflower oil
1 cup coconut milk (either powder and water or tinned)

1 pack Thai curry herbs from the supermarket or
2 red and 2 green very small chilli peppers or $\frac{1}{2}$ to
    1 teaspoon chilli powder
Small bunch fresh coriander
2 or 3 lemon grass stems
2 lime leaves

2 sheets of noodles from a packet of medium noodles
1 tablespoon sesame oil

EQUIPMENT

Garlic crusher
Sharp knife
Chopping board
Zester or grater
Juicer
Saucepan
Set of measuring spoons
Wok or frying-pan
Wooden spoon
Set of measuring cups

METHOD

Peel and crush the garlic. Chop the chicken into bite-sized pieces. De-seed and chop the chilli peppers. Wash, dry and chop the coriander leaves. Peel, slice and chop the ginger. Zest the lime and juice it. Use a grater or a sharp knife if you don't have a zester. Hit the lemon grass so the stems begin to separate but do not fall apart.

Fill the saucepan with water and bring to the boil.

Meantime, put the sunflower oil into the frying-pan. Add the garlic, ginger, lime zest, lime leaves, chopped chillies, the lemon grass and stir for 2–3 minutes. Add the chopped chicken and stir so that it is evenly coated and the flavours are spread equally. Cook for approximately 7 minutes.

Add the lime juice and stir and cook for 1–2 minutes. Add the coconut milk. When the coconut milk has reduced by about half add the noodles to the boiling water, turn off the heat and cover the saucepan.

Meantime continue to stir the chicken and the coconut milk.

Check how long the noodles take on the packet. They will probably need about 4 or 5 minutes. When the noodles are cooked, drain and then return them to the saucepan, add the sesame oil and toss the noodles so that they get coated. Pick out the lemon grass stems and lime leaves, and add the coriander leaves. Pile the noodles on to the plates and pile the chicken on top.

ADDITIONS & ALTERNATIVES

Serve with soy sauce and sliced spring onion if desired.

Instead of chicken use bite-sized pieces of pork or beef or white fish.

Serve with rice instead of noodles.

TIPS

Prepared garlic is sold in tubes and jars. Just read the tube or jar for the suggested equivalent amount. It keeps for six weeks in the fridge.

Prepared lemon grass is available dried or in jars. It will keep in the fridge for six weeks.

Chillies are available in jars or tubes. It keeps for six weeks in the fridge.

SPECIAL FRIED RICE

Serves 2 to 3   ① *Preparation 5 min, Cooking 5 min – Moderate, it helps if someone can put the rice in the wok while you beat the eggs*

INGREDIENTS

2 or 3 cups cooked rice
$\frac{1}{2}$ cup frozen peas
$\frac{1}{2}$ cup frozen sweet corn (optional)
$\frac{1}{2}$ cup or more frozen prawns (optional)
100 to 200 g (4 to 8 oz) cooked chicken, or cup of left-over chicken
4 spring onions
2 eggs
2 tablespoons oil

EQUIPMENT

Saucepan
Set of measuring cups
Sharp knife
Chopping board

Bowl
Fork
Set of measuring spoons
Frying-pan or wok
Wooden spoon

METHOD

If you are cooking the rice, follow the instructions on the packet. There are full instructions on cooking rice in the 'How to' chapter.

Thaw the frozen ingredients in cold water and drain them.

Shred the cooked chicken. Clean and prepare the spring onions. Cut the root end off, trim the leaves. Peel off and discard any dried up or slimy leaves. Chop roughly. Break the eggs into a bowl. Fish out any bits of shell then whisk the eggs with a fork.

Heat the oil in a wok. Pour the eggs in the wok and stir round for 30 seconds. This is the bit where an assistant may help. Keep stirring and put in the rice. Stir fry, breaking up the rice with the spoon. Stir until the rice grains separate (less than 5 minutes). Add the other ingredients and stir for a couple of minutes until they are warmed through then serve.

ADDITIONS & ALTERNATIVES

This is a meal on its own. Serve with soy sauce.

Add chopped sweet pepper.

Use chopped cooked left-over beef or pork instead of the chicken or leave out the meat altogether.

CHINESE SPARE RIBS

Serves 3 to 4 ① *Preparation 5 min, Cooking 90 min – Moderate*

INGREDIENTS
1 kg (2 lbs) spare ribs, separated
½ bottle (150 ml) Hoi Sin sauce

EQUIPMENT
Bowl
Ovenproof dish
Aluminium foil

METHOD
Put the Hoi Sin sauce in a bowl then add the ribs. Stir them round so they are coated. Put the ribs in the ovenproof dish and cover with foil. Cook in a preheated oven for 90 minutes at 180°C, 350°F, Gas mark 4.

ADDITIONS & ALTERNATIVES
Serve with rice
   Grill the ribs for 25 minutes, turning them often.

TIPS
You can use this recipe for a barbecue.

ITALIAN

ANTIPASTI

Serves 2 or 4   ① *Preparation 3 min – Easy but expensive*

INGREDIENTS
Jars of antipasti
Sun-dried tomatoes
Mushrooms
Italian mixed vegetables
Artichoke hearts
Aubergines
Courgettes
Olives
Bread

EQUIPMENT
Plate

METHOD
Open the jars and fish out the vegetables. Arrange tastefully on a plate. Serve with crusty bread or Italian bread.

TOASTED ROASTED PEPPERS

A plate full   ⏱ *Preparation 5 min, Cooking 15 min – Easy*

INGREDIENTS
2 or 3 large ripe red peppers
1 tablespoon olive oil

EQUIPMENT
Sharp knife
Chopping board
Grill
Set of measuring spoons

METHOD
What you are aiming for are soft, sweet, cooked, peeled, red pepper.

Wash and dry the peppers. Cut the peppers in half. Remove the seeds and the central white bit under the stalk.

Turn the grill on full. Put the pepper on the grill tray skin side down and cook for a couple of minutes. Turn them over and cook for another couple of minutes. The skins will go brown and start to bubble up.

Take the peppers from under the grill and allow to cool. Slide the burnt skin off. Put the peppers on a plate and pour the oil over them.

ADDITIONS & ALTERNATIVES
Serve as a starter or as a snack with other bits like cheese, olives, salami and chorizo (spiced, sliced sausage).

GRILLED COURGETTES

Starter for 4   ① *Preparation 5 min, Cooking 15 min – Easy*

INGREDIENTS
4 courgettes
4 cloves garlic
1 dried chilli
4 tablespoons olive oil
1 tablespoon of white wine vinegar

EQUIPMENT
Sharp knife
Chopping board
Grill
Bowl
Set of measuring spoons
Wooden spoon

METHOD
Wash the courgettes and cut off the top and bottom. Cut into four slices lengthways. Cook under a hot grill for about ten minutes each side. When they are brown turn them over. It is OK if they go quite black in places.

Meanwhile peel and cut the garlic into small pieces. Carefully chop the dried whole chilli. Put the courgette in the bowl. Add the garlic, chilli, oil and vinegar. Stir and refrigerate.

ADDITIONS & ALTERNATIVES
Serve with Italian bread and other antipasti.

ITALIAN ROAST CHICKEN

Serves 4   ① *Preparation 10 min, Cooking 35 min*
(can increase quantities)   *– Easy and impressive*

INGREDIENTS
8–12 chicken thighs
3 tablespoons of olive oil
1 bunch fresh rosemary or 3 tablespoons dried
Salt and freshly ground pepper to taste
3 cloves garlic
1 kg (2 lbs) small new potatoes
Lettuce, tomato, spring onion, olives, etc. for salad
Italian bread (optional). There is a recipe for Focaccia on page 261.

EQUIPMENT
Set of measuring spoons
2 roasting tins or ovenproof dishes
Sharp knife
Chopping board
1 wooden spoon
Potato peeler

METHOD
Make sure frozen chicken is completely thawed before use. This means leaving it in the fridge overnight, or out of the fridge, covered, for six hours.

Turn the oven on at 200°C, 400°F, Gas mark 6. Put half the oil in each roasting tin. Break the rosemary leaves off the stem (or open the jar). Put the chicken pieces in one of the roasting dishes. Add half the rosemary. Mix with the spoon so that the chicken is coated in oil and rosemary. Add a little salt (half a teaspoon) and pepper. Peel and chop the garlic. Put in the dish with the chicken.

Wash the potatoes. Peel them if you have to. Cut off any nasty bits and sprouts. Cut the potatoes into 1 cm (half-inch) slices. Put the potatoes into the other roasting dish. Add the rest of the rosemary and mix so the potatoes are covered in oil and rosemary. Add a little (half a teaspoon) fresh ground salt.

Put both roasting dishes in the oven for 30–35 minutes, until the potatoes are golden and the chicken is golden and cooked.

ADDITIONS & ALTERNATIVES
Serve with salad and Italian bread.

Use chicken breasts or legs instead of thighs. Add 5–10 minutes to the cooking time if you are using larger pieces.

Roast fresh baby sweet corn or small onions in with the chicken.

ITALIAN ROAST LAMB

Serves 4 (can   ① *Preparation 10 min,*
increase quantities)   *Cooking 35 min – Easy and impressive*

INGREDIENTS
8–12 mini lamb chops instead of chicken pieces in the previous recipe

METHOD
Substitute the mini lamb chops for the chicken pieces in the recipe above.

ADDITIONS & ALTERNATIVES
Mini lamb chops come from the supermarket freezer cabinet.

TOMATO SAUCE

Enough for spaghetti for 2   ① *Preparation 5 min,*
Cooking 10 min – Easy

INGREDIENTS
2 medium onions
2 tablespoons olive oil
3 cloves garlic
400 g tin Italian plum tomatoes
1–2 teaspoons oregano, mixed herbs or mixed Mediterranean herbs
Salt and freshly ground pepper to taste

EQUIPMENT
Sharp knife
Chopping board
Set of measuring spoons
Frying-pan
Wooden spoon
Tin opener

METHOD
Peel the onion and cut into thin slices, then chop across so you end up with small bits.

Put the oil in the frying-pan and put on a medium heat. Peel and crush the garlic into the pan. Fry the garlic and the onion on a medium heat for about two minutes. Stir them every half a minute or so.

Open the tin of tomatoes. Pour the juice into the frying-pan. Use the wooden spoon to mash the tomatoes while they are still in the can (it's easier than chasing them round the pan). Pour the mashed tomatoes into the pan. Continue to cook, stirring as the mixture boils. Add your chosen herb, oregano being most authentic. Season with salt and pepper. Cook for another five minutes and serve.

ADDITIONS & ALTERNATIVES

The sauce can be made even better by adding a glass of wine and cooking a bit longer.

TIPS

This sauce is the basis of a whole load of Italian food. It is great on spaghetti with Parmesan cheese.

It is the basis of the sauce for Bolognese and the meat sauce for Lasagne, and their vegetarian versions.

It is a tomato sauce for pizza.

BOLOGNESE SAUCE

Enough for spaghetti for 2   ⓘ *Preparation 5 min,*
                                         Cooking 12 min – Easy

INGREDIENTS

2 medium onions
1 tablespoon olive oil
3 cloves garlic
500 g (1 lb) beef mince
400 g tin Italian plum tomatoes
1 beef stock cube
1–2 teaspoons oregano, mixed herbs or mixed Mediterranean herbs
Salt and freshly ground pepper to taste

EQUIPMENT

Sharp knife
Chopping board
Set of measuring spoons
Frying-pan

Wooden spoon
Tin opener

METHOD

Peel the onion and cut into thin slices, then chop across so you end up with small bits. Put the oil in the frying-pan and put on a medium heat. Peel and crush the garlic into the pan. Fry the garlic and the onion on a medium heat for about two minutes. Stir them every half a minute or so.

Put the meat in the frying-pan and fry for two or three minutes, stirring all the time. By this time it should have broken up and be an even colour, with no pink bits.

Open the tin of tomatoes. Pour the juice into the frying-pan. Crumble the stock cube into the pan. Use the wooden spoon to mash the tomatoes while they are still in the can (it's easier than chasing them round the pan). Pour the mashed tomatoes into the pan. Continue to cook, stirring as the mixture boils. Add your chosen herb, oregano being authentic. Season with salt and pepper. Cook for another five minutes or so until the fluid has reduced and the sauce is less sloppy.

ADDITIONS & ALTERNATIVES

Serve with spaghetti or other pasta. Just follow the cooking time on the packet. There are full instructions on cooking pasta in the 'How to' chapter. The sauce can be improved by adding a glass of wine and cooking a bit longer. The vegetarian version of this uses soya mince instead of the meat. Read the pack instructions, but in general it tastes as good, and is quicker to cook.

TIPS

Mince quality and price are related. The cheaper the mince the more fat, the less meat, the more colouring, and odd bits you may not consider as actual 'meat'. The best stuff is made by buying a cheap cut of beef and getting the butcher to mince it up. That way you know what you're getting.

TUNA MAYONNAISE PASTA

Serves 2   ① *Preparation 5 min, Cooking 5 to 15 min – Easy*

INGREDIENTS

200 g tin tuna
2 or 3 spring onions
2 tablespoons mayonnaise
Freshly ground pepper
250 g (half a packet) pasta shapes
1 or 2 tablespoons grated Parmesan cheese

EQUIPMENT

Tin opener
Bowl
Fork
Sharp knife
Chopping board
Set of measuring spoons
Saucepan

METHOD

Open the tin of tuna. Drain the liquid from the tin. Put the tuna in the bowl and mash it up with the fork.

Get the spring onions and take off the outer leaves. Cut off the root end and trim off the green leaves and any other unsavoury bits. Wash the spring onions and dry. Shred the onions into thin rings with the knife. Put the onions and the mayonnaise in with the tuna and mix up. Add pepper, if you wish.

Read the pasta packet to give you the cooking time (somewhere between 5 and 15 minutes). Put at least a pint of water and a teaspoon of salt in the saucepan. Bring to the boil and add the pasta. Stir once. When the pasta is cooked, drain it and put it in the bowl. Add the tuna mayonnaise and mix round.

ADDITIONS & ALTERNATIVES

Serve sprinkled with grated Parmesan cheese and freshly ground pepper, and with fresh warm bread and salad.

TIPS

There are full instructions on cooking pasta in the 'How to' chapter.

PASTA & BACON

Serves 2   ① *Preparation 3 min, cooking 10 min – Easy*

INGREDIENTS

Half pack of pasta shells (250 g)
2 or more cloves garlic
1 or 2 medium onions
1 pack streaky bacon (about 6 to 8 rashers)
1 tablespoon olive oil
10 mushrooms (100 g or 4 oz) (optional)
Salt and freshly ground pepper to taste
2 tablespoons Parmesan cheese

EQUIPMENT

Saucepan
Sharp knife
Chopping board
Set of measuring spoons
Frying-pan
Wooden spoon

METHOD

Put at least a pint of water and a teaspoon of salt in the saucepan. Bring to the boil. Put in the pasta, cooking according to the instructions on the packet. Stir it once to stop it sticking to the pan.

Peel and chop the garlic and the onions. Chop the bacon. Put the oil in the frying-pan. Fry the bacon for about 3 minutes, stirring from time to time. Add the onions and garlic. Fry for another couple of minutes. Keep on stirring. Add the mushrooms if you like and cook for another minute or so. Season with salt and pepper. Strain the pasta and put it together with the bacon mixture in a bowl. Serve with Parmesan cheese.

TIPS

Work out the timing so it is all ready at about the same time. Read the cooking instructions on the packet of pasta shapes. They will need boiling for between 5 and 15 minutes. The bacon takes about 5 minutes. If the bacon is cooked too soon, just take it off the heat and warm it up when the pasta is cooked.

Serve with salad.

PASTA WITH BROCCOLI & CHILLI

Serves 2   ① *Preparation 5 min, Cooking 6 to 15 min – Easy*

INGREDIENTS

250 g (half a packet) of pasta shapes, orchetti, shells or similar
Medium head of broccoli (300 g or 10 oz)
2 cloves garlic
2 tablespoons olive oil
$\frac{1}{2}$ teaspoon hot chilli powder
2 tablespoons grated Parmesan cheese

EQUIPMENT

Saucepan
Sharp knife

Chopping board
Set of measuring spoons
Frying-pan
Wooden spoon
Bowl

METHOD

Read the pasta packet to get the cooking time (anything between 5 and 15 minutes). Put at least a pint of water with a teaspoon of salt in the saucepan, bring to the boil. Put the pasta in the water. Stir once to stop it sticking to the pan. Bring back to the boil.

Break the broccoli into little bits (florets). Peel and chop the garlic.

Meanwhile, put the oil in the frying-pan and fry the garlic and chilli powder for a minute or so. Add the broccoli and stir round so that the broccoli is covered in the garlic, chilli and oil. Keep stirring and frying till it is cooked, about three to five minutes. Take off the heat.

Drain the pasta. Stir the pasta and broccoli together in a bowl. Put two tablespoons of grated Parmesan on top.

ADDITIONS & ALTERNATIVES

Serve with salad

Substitute Pecorino cheese for Parmesan.

Add chopped tinned anchovies sprinkled on the top when serving.

Substitute mange tout, French beans or cauliflower for the broccoli.

CARBONARA HAM PASTA SAUCE

Serves 2   ⓘ *Preparation 5 min, Cooking 5 min – Easy*

INGREDIENTS

2 cloves garlic
1 medium onion
10 mushrooms (about 100 g or 4 oz)
3 slices of cooked ham
1 tablespoon olive oil
1 tablespoon flour
Small carton (142 ml or 5 fl oz) single cream
1 teaspoon of mixed Mediterranean herbs
Salt and freshly ground pepper to taste
250 g packet tagliatelli

EQUIPMENT

Sharp knife
Chopping board
Frying-pan
Saucepan
Wooden spoon
Garlic crusher
Set of measuring spoons

METHOD

Peel and crush the garlic. Peel the onion and slice thinly. Wipe the mushrooms to get any dirt off and then slice them. Cut the ham up into 1 cm (half-inch) squares.

Heat oil in frying-pan. Add the onion and garlic. Cook till the onion has gone soft, about a couple of minutes, stirring so they cook evenly. Add the mushrooms, stir and cook for a couple of minutes more. Add the ham. Add the flour and stir round until it has absorbed the oil and juices in the pan. Add the cream, the herbs and some salt and pepper. Stir round and cook for about a minute until it has made a smooth sauce and serve with pasta (see below for cooking instructions).

ADDITIONS & ALTERNATIVES

Try bacon instead of ham. Chop the bacon up and fry it with the onions. This adds a couple of minutes to the cooking time. You can buy this sauce ready made.

TIPS

Prepared garlic is sold in tubes and jars. Just read the tube or jar for the suggested equivalent amount. It keeps for six weeks in the fridge.

The best pasta for this is tagliatelli, which takes about three to five minutes to cook. Read the packet for the correct time. Anyway this works out quite well, just boil the water for the tagliatelli while you are chopping up the onion and the rest. Then throw the pasta in the water when you have cooked the onions. The sauce will be cooked before you need to drain the pasta, just take it off the heat, check the pasta is cooked, drain it and serve.

PASTA WITH PESTO

Serves 2   ① *Preparation 1 min, Cooking 5 to 15 min – Easy*

INGREDIENTS
250 g (half a packet) pasta shapes
2 tablespoons pesto
1 tablespoon olive oil

EQUIPMENT
Saucepan
Bowl
Set of measuring spoons

METHOD
Read the pasta packet to give you the cooking time (somewhere between 5 and 15 minutes). Put at least a pint of water and a teaspoon of salt in the saucepan. Bring to the boil and add the pasta. When the pasta is cooked, drain it and put it in the bowl. Add the pesto and olive oil and mix round.

ADDITIONS & ALTERNATIVES
Serve immediately, with salad and bread.

Pesto is a sauce made from basil among other things, available in green and red.

TIPS
There are full instructions on cooking pasta in the 'How to' chapter.

LEMON SEAFOOD & ANGEL'S HAIR PASTA

2 generous portions   ① *Preparation 20 min, Cooking 15 min*
– Moderate

INGREDIENTS
6 mushrooms
1 small/medium broccoli head
2 courgettes
1 lemon
4–6 small ready prepared squid tubes
2 tablespoons sunflower oil
1 tablespoon olive oil
3 cloves garlic
$\frac{1}{3}$ × 500 g packet dried Angel's Hair (or other fine pasta)
10–16 large cooked and shelled prawns (can use frozen ones)
Salt and black pepper to taste

EQUIPMENT
Sharp knife
Chopping board
Lemon zester or grater
Lemon juicer
Large saucepan
Set of measuring spoons
Large frying-pan
Garlic crusher
Wooden spoon or spatula
Sieve to drain pasta

METHOD
Wipe and slice mushrooms. Rinse the broccoli and break it into florets. Slice the florets up. Rinse and slice the courgettes. Peel the skin off the lemon in thin strips with the zester or a knife. Juice

the lemon. Slice the squid into 1 cm (half-inch) rings. Cut the tentacles in half. Fill the saucepan with water and put on to boil.

Put the oil into the frying-pan, and put on a medium heat. When the oil is warm crush the garlic into the frying-pan, add the lemon zest, and cook gently for 2 minutes. Add the squid rings and cook for 5 minutes. Add the broccoli and courgettes.

Put the pasta into the saucepan and bring the water back to the boil. Once boiled it will take 3 minutes to cook.

Add the sliced mushrooms, prawns and lemon juice to the frying-pan. Reduce the heat, stir occasionally, and cook for 3 minutes.

Drain the water from the pasta. Combine the pasta with the seafood and vegetables and serve.

ADDITIONS & ALTERNATIVES

Serve with white wine, Italian bread and mixed salad leaves.

Use other vegetables instead of courgettes and broccoli, like French beans, asparagus, cauliflower or sliced green pepper.

Use other seafood, such as scallops, clams or mussels, small pieces of fish or even small fish like whitebait, fresh anchovies or fresh sardines.

Use other fine pasta like tagliattellini, or fine spaghetti. These will take longer to cook so check the time on the packet and adjust when you put them on to boil.

TIPS

Squid tubes are stocked by supermarkets and some fishmongers. Don't buy unprepared squid unless you like slimy things and know how to take the quill out. But check the prepared ones, as you chop them, for a strip of clear plastic like stuff. If you find it, throw it away. It is the quill.

Prepared garlic is sold in tubes and jars. Just read the tube or jar for the suggested equivalent amount. It keeps for six weeks in the fridge.

LASAGNE

Serves 6   ⏱ *Preparation 15 min, cooking 60 min – Moderate*

INGREDIENTS
1 *quantity of Bolognese sauce*
1 tablespoon olive oil
3 cloves of garlic
2 medium onions
500 g (1 lb) beef mince
400 g tin Italian plum tomatoes
1 beef stock cube
1–2 teaspoons oregano, mixed herbs or mixed Mediterranean herbs
Salt and freshly ground pepper to taste

250 g packet of lasagne pasta (look for 'no pre-cooking required' on the packet)
Parmesan cheese

White sauce
4 tablespoons butter
6 tablespoons flour
2 cups milk (500 ml or 1 pint)
1–2 tablespoons grated Parmesan cheese
Salt and freshly ground pepper to taste

EQUIPMENT
Sharp knife
Chopping board
Large ovenproof dish (2 litre or 3 ½ pints)
Frying-pan
Saucepan
Wooden spoon

Tin opener
Set of measuring spoons
Set of measuring cups

METHOD

To make the Bolognese sauce

Put the oil in the frying-pan. Peel and crush the garlic. Peel and chop the onions. Fry the garlic and chopped onion on a medium heat for about two minutes. Stir them every half a minute or so.

Put the meat in the frying-pan and fry for two or three minutes, stirring all the time. By this time it should have broken up and be an even colour, with no pink bits.

Open the tin of tomatoes. Pour the juice into the frying-pan. Crumble stock cube into pan. Use the wooden spoon to mash the tomatocs while they are still in the can (it's easier than chasing them round the pan). Pour the mashed tomatoes into the pan. Continue to cook, stirring as the mixture boils. Add your chosen herb, oregano being authentic. Season with salt and pepper. Cook for another five minutes or so until the fluid has reduced and the sauce is less sloppy.

The sauce can be improved by adding a glass of wine and cooking a bit longer.

To make the white sauce

Melt the butter in a saucepan over a low heat. Add flour and stir together to make a smooth paste. Take the pan off the heat. Continue to stir and add the milk a bit at a time. If you add it too quickly it will go lumpy. When all the milk has been added, put it back on the heat and gently bring to the boil, stirring all the time, until thickened. Add one or two tablespoons of Parmesan cheese. Season with salt and pepper.

Assemble the lasagne in the ovenproof dish

Start with a layer of Bolognese sauce. Cover with a layer of lasagne pasta. Then a layer of Bolognese sauce. Next a layer of white sauce. Then pasta, Bolognese, white sauce.

However many layers you do, it must end up with white sauce on top. Sprinkle the top with Parmesan cheese.

Cook in a preheated oven at 180°C, 350°F, Gas mark 4 for about 30 minutes. The top should be golden brown.

ADDITIONS & ALTERNATIVES

Use prepared Bolognese sauce from the supermarket.

TIPS

Prepared garlic is sold in tubes and jars. Just read the tube or jar for the suggested equivalent amount. It keeps for six weeks in the fridge.

RISOTTO

Serves 4   ① *Preparation 5 min, Cooking 20 to 25 min*
Needs an eye keeping on it all the time

INGREDIENTS

1 medium onion
3–4 cloves garlic
3 tablespoons olive oil
400–500 g (about 1 lb) of one of the following:
    minced beef, chopped chicken, frozen vegetables, prawns
1 cup risotto rice
227 g tin chopped tomatoes
2 tablespoons parsley
$\frac{1}{2}$ cup of wine
1 $\frac{1}{2}$ cups water or stock
Salt

EQUIPMENT
Sharp knife
Chopping board
Large saucepan
Set of measuring spoons
Wooden spoon
Set of measuring cups
Tin opener

METHOD
Peel and chop the onion and the garlic. Put the oil in a large saucepan. Fry the onion a minute or so then add the mince, chicken, vegetables or prawns and fry for a further three minutes or so.

Add the rice and fry for another couple of minutes. Add the garlic, tomatoes, parsley, wine, stock and salt to taste. Simmer for 20–25 minutes, until the fluid is absorbed and the rice is cooked. If it looks like it is getting dry, add some more water or wine and give it a stir.

ADDITIONS & ALTERNATIVES
This dish needs watching to make sure it cooks but stays moist.

FOCACCIA BREAD

Serves 4 ① *Preparation 15 min plus 20 and 30 minutes to rise, Cooking 25 min – Moderately strenuous, but worth it*

INGREDIENTS
2 cups (250 g or half a small bag) plain white flour
Coarse sea salt
2 teaspoons easy blend dried yeast
3 tablespoons olive oil
150 ml (10 tablespoons) warm water
and, if you like, one or more of the following:
A few leaves of fresh rosemary
6 cloves of garlic
10 olives
3 sun dried tomatoes

EQUIPMENT
Sieve
Mixing bowl
Set of measuring spoons
Wooden spoon
1 clean tea towel or some cling film
Baking tray

METHOD
Sieve the flour and 1 teaspoon of salt into the mixing bowl. If there is no sieve, break up any lumps with a fork. Add the easy blend yeast. Mix again. Make a well in the middle of the flour.

Mix a tablespoon of olive oil and the warm water, and pour it into the flour mixture. Use the wooden spoon to mix the dough. Try to get rid of any lumps of dry flour and keep at it till the dough becomes less sticky and comes away from the side of the bowl.

261

Now knead the dough. This is a process of stretching the dough and then folding it back on itself, rather than hitting it. It makes the gluten in the flour develop, and makes the springy texture which lets the bubbles of gas make the bread rise. Form the dough into a ball. Sprinkle some flour on a firm, clean, dry surface, like a bread board or kitchen surface. Alternatively, knead it in the bowl. Use the heel of the hand to push half the dough away. Fold it over, turn it round a bit and repeat until the dough is springy and smooth. This is much easier to do than to describe. Knead for about ten minutes.

Put the dough back in the bowl. Cover the bowl with something clean and damp, like a tea towel. Failing being able to locate a tea towel, use cling film. Put the bowl somewhere warm for about twenty minutes. The dough should have doubled in size. Take the towel/cling film off. Hit the top of the dough. It should collapse as you knock the air out of it.

Wipe the baking tray with a little oil. Stretch out the dough using your fingers so it ends up about half to one centimetre (quarter to half an inch) thick. Cover the dough with that damp tea towel or cling film again and leave for half an hour. It will have expanded a bit.

Gently push your fingertip into the surface in several places, so it becomes deeply dimpled. Brush or dribble the olive oil on the top. Sprinkle 2 teaspoons of coarse (unground) sea salt on top.

Rosemary is the standard garnish, but olives, garlic or sun-dried tomatoes are very good.

Cook in a preheated oven at 220°C, 425°F, Gas mark 7 for about 20 to 25 minutes. Allow to cool but eat while warm if possible.

ADDITIONS & ALTERNATIVES

This looks a bit like pizza, and the dough is exactly the same. It is also the dough for Calzoni, a kind of inside-out pizza, great for packed meals.

TIPS

There are three kinds of yeast. Fresh yeast comes from health food shops. It will keep in the fridge for a few days but will eventually die.

Dried yeast comes in tubs from the supermarket. It, like fresh yeast, needs to be 'activated' before use, by adding it to warm water, often with a teaspoon of sugar. There are generally instructions on the packet.

Easy to blend yeast comes in packets from the supermarket. It can be mixed straight in with the flour.

PIZZA

Makes 2 pizzas   ① *Preparation 5 min for bought pizza bases,*
(8 to 12 slices)   *15 minutes otherwise, Cooking 20 min*
  – Easy if you use bought bases, moderate if you make your own

INGREDIENTS
1 quantity Focaccia dough (see previous recipe)
   or bought pizza bases
400 g tin Italian plum tomatoes
150 g Mozzarella cheese
1–2 teaspoons oregano
Choose toppings from:
salami, tuna, sliced tomatoes, anchovies, olives, capers, mushrooms, red sweet pepper slices, sweet corn, ham and pineapple,
sardines.

EQUIPMENT
Baking tray
Tin opener
Wooden spoon
Sharp knife
Chopping board

METHOD
Make the Focaccia dough, just like in the last recipe, except divide
it in two, and roll it out into circles on the baking sheet. Or buy
pizza bases. If you are using bought bases read the packet carefully
and cook according to their instructions. The cooking times here
are for pizza made with fresh dough.

  Drain the tomatoes. Squeeze two tomatoes through your
fingers on to each pizza. Spread the layer with a spoon. Sprinkle
with oregano. Put your chosen topping on top. Cover with slices

of mozzarella cheese. Cook in a preheated oven at 240°C, 475°F, Gas mark 9 for 10 to 15 minutes.

ADDITIONS & ALTERNATIVES

Use the tomato sauce on page 245, bought tomato pizza sauce or even tomato paste instead of the tomato sauce.

Use Cheddar cheese instead of Mozzarella.

TIPS

Shops sell ready shredded Mozzarella cheese.

Great party food. Double quantities will make 4 pizzas for 16 to 24 slices.

MEAT CALZONI

Serves 4   ① *Preparation 15 min plus 40 minutes rising time,*
Cooking 15 to 20 min – Moderate

INGREDIENTS

1 quantity Focaccia dough (page 261)
1 medium onion
1 tablespoon olive oil
2 tinned plum tomatoes
50 g (2 oz) Italian sausage or salami
2 slices of cooked ham
1 tablespoon chopped parsley
100 g Mozzarella cheese

EQUIPMENT

Sharp knife
Chopping board
Set of measuring spoons
Frying-pan
Tin opener
Rolling pin

METHOD

Make the Focaccia dough from the previous recipe, mixing, kneading and allowing it to rise for about 20 minutes till it has doubled in size. While waiting for the dough to rise, make the filling.

Meat filling: peel and chop the onion. Put the oil in the frying-pan. Gently fry the onion for about three to five minutes, until it goes soft. Take the frying-pan off the heat. Open the tin of tomatoes. Drain the tomatoes. Put them into the frying-pan, and mash them up. Chop the sausage and the ham. Put them into the pan with the parsley.

Knock the dough down and give it another brief knead. Divide the dough into four pieces. Roll it out or flatten it to about the size of a small plate about 15 cm (6 inches) across. Divide up the filling into 4 and put it into the middle of each circle. Chop the Mozzarclla into cubes and divide it up between the Calzonis. Fold over the dough sealing the edge with a little water. Brush each Calzoni with a little olive oil. Smear some oil on a baking sheet. Put the Calzoni on the baking sheet. Wait about 15 minutes for the dough to rise a little. Cook in a preheated oven at 220°C, 425°F, Gas mark 7 for about 15 to 20 minutes.

VEGETABLE CALZONI

Serves 4   ⓘ *Preparation 15 min plus 40 minutes rising time, Cooking 15 to 20 min – Moderate*

INGREDIENTS
1 quantity Focaccia dough

Vegetable filling
4 cloves of garlic
1 medium onion
1 red sweet pepper
1 tablespoon olive oil
400 g tin of artichoke hearts
tinned plum tomatoes
2 tablespoons Parmesan cheese
2 tablespoons parsley
100 g Mozzarella cheese

EQUIPMENT
Sharp knife
Chopping board
Garlic crusher
Set of measuring spoons
Frying-pan
Tin opener
Rolling pin

METHOD
Follow the instructions in the previous recipe for dough and preparation but use vegetable filling instead of meat.

Vegetable filling: Peel and crush the garlic. Peel and chop the onion. Chop the red pepper, throwing away the core and seeds.

Put the oil in the frying-pan. Gently fry the garlic, onion and sweet pepper for about three to five minutes, until the onion goes soft. Take the frying pan off the heat.

Open the tins of artichoke hearts and tomatoes. Drain the tomatoes. Put them into the frying-pan, and mash them up. Mix in the Parmesan cheese. Chop the artichoke hearts and put them into the pan. Add the parsley. Put the mixture on to the dough. Chop the Mozzarella into cubes and divide it up between the Calzonis.

FISH CALZONI

Serves 4   ⏲ *Preparation 15 min plus 40 minutes rising time, Cooking 15 to 20 min – Moderate*

INGREDIENTS
1 quantity Focaccia dough
3–4 cloves garlic

1 medium onion
1 tablespoon olive oil
200 g tin tuna
2 tinned plum tomatoes
100 g tin clams (optional)
2 tablespoons fresh parsley
100 g Mozzarella cheese

EQUIPMENT
Sharp knife
Chopping board
Garlic crusher
Set of measuring spoons
Frying-pan
Tin opener
Rolling pin

METHOD
Follow the instructions in the previous recipe for the dough and preparation but use fish filling instead of meat or vegetables.

Peel and crush the garlic. Peel and chop the onion. Put the oil in the frying-pan. Gently fry the garlic and onion for about three to five minutes, until the onion goes soft. Take the frying-pan off the heat.

Open the tins of tuna, tomatoes and clams. Drain the tomatoes. Put them into the frying- pan, and mash them up. Put the tuna, parsley and clams into the pan. Put the mixture on to the dough. Chop the Mozzarella into cubes and divide it up between the Calzonis.

GUACAMOLE

Serves 2   ① *Preparation 5 min – Easy*

INGREDIENTS
2 ripe avocados
1 large ripe tomato
1 tablespoon lemon juice
$\frac{1}{2}$ to 1 teaspoon chilli powder
    or 1 or 2 fresh shredded chillies with the seeds removed
Salt and freshly ground pepper to taste

EQUIPMENT
Sharp knife
Chopping board
Bowl
Fork for mashing
Set of measuring spoons

METHOD
Ripe avocados mash easily. Cut the avocados in half, peel and remove the stone. Mash the avocado with a fork.

Peel the tomato, chop in half, take out the seeds and chop up small. *To peel tomatoes*: make a cut in the shape of a cross in the base and top of the tomato. Drop into a saucepan of boiling water for 30 seconds. Pour the boiling water away and cover with cold water. When it's cool enough to touch, the skin should slide off easily.

Mash all the ingredients together. Serve as a dip for crisps, taco chips, nachos, or with other salads.

TIPS

FRESH CHILLI – A WARNING! When you chop up the chillies be careful and avoid getting juice on your hands. If you touch your eyes, mouth or other sensitive areas even an hour after chopping them they will smart and burn. So wash your hands or wear rubber gloves.

Prepared chilli is sold in tubes and jars. Just read the tube or jar for the suggested equivalent amount. It keeps for six weeks in the fridge.

BARBECUE SAUCE

For barbecues or meat   ⏱ *Preparation 2 min,*
                                           Cooking 2 min – Easy

INGREDIENTS
2 tablespoons butter
1 tablespoon sugar
3 tablespoons tomato ketchup
2 tablespoons HP sauce
1 tablespoon Worcestershire sauce (Lea and Perrins)
1 tablespoon mushroom ketchup (if you can find it)
2 drops Tabasco

EQUIPMENT
Saucepan
Wooden spoon
Set of measuring spoons

METHOD
Melt the butter with the sugar in the pan over a low heat. Take the pan off the heat. Add the ketchup, HP sauce, Worcestershire sauce, mushroom ketchup and the Tabasco. Mix it all together. Ready to serve.

ADDITIONS & ALTERNATIVES
Try fruity brown sauces, whatever you have, instead of the brown sauce.

TIPS
This is a multipurpose sauce. You can cook with it, or use it as a sauce with barbecue burgers or sausages.

This will keep in the fridge for 48 hours.

Use this as a marinade and sauce for spare ribs (recipe below).

TEXAN BARBECUED SPARE RIBS

Serves 3 to 4   ① *Preparation 5 min, Cooking 25 min – Easy*

INGREDIENTS
1 kg (2 lbs) spare ribs, separated
1 quantity barbecue sauce (as above)

EQUIPMENT
Bowl
Wooden spoon
Grill
Cooking tongs

METHOD
Put two-thirds of the barbecue sauce in a bowl then add the ribs. Stir them round so they are coated. Preferably leave for a couple of hours.

Turn on the grill. Put the ribs on the grill on edge. As you will notice the meat on a rib is at the edges and the knobbly end. This is the bit that needs cooking. The hassle of this is that you need to keep an eye on them, turning them over and moving the cooked ones to the edge. Think of it as a barbecue.

ADDITIONS & ALTERNATIVES
You can serve this without anything other than the remaining barbecue sauce, or serve with boiled rice and salad.

There is not much meat on a spare rib.

Use this recipe for a barbecue.

FRESH COOKED POTATO SKINS

Starter for 4   ① *Preparation 5 min, Cooking 20 min – Easy*

INGREDIENTS
3 large potatoes
Sunflower oil
1 medium carton (284 ml or 10 fl oz) sour cream
1 pack fresh chives

EQUIPMENT
Sharp knife
Chopping board
Frying-pan
Wooden spoon
Bowl

METHOD
Take a potato and wash it. Cut it into quarters or eighths (a bit like following the seams on a rugby ball). Cut away half the potato flesh.

Fry skins in sunflower oil for about 5 to 10 minutes until done. Lift out the skins and drain on kitchen roll. You can keep them warm in the oven while you cook the rest.

Wash, dry and chop the chives. Put the sour cream in the bowl. Add the chives. Stir. Serve with the fried potato skins.

ADDITIONS & ALTERNATIVES
Try with other dips like Guacamole (page 270) or Fresh Mexican Salsa (page 276). You can buy a wide range of sauces and dips in jars.

BOUGHT POTATO SKINS

Starter for 4   ① *Preparation 3 min, Cooking 15 min – Easy*

INGREDIENTS
250 g pack frozen potato skins
1 medium carton (284 ml or 10 fl oz) sour cream
1 pack fresh chives

EQUIPMENT
Baking sheet
Sharp knife
Chopping board
Bowl
Wooden spoon

METHOD
Read the instructions on the frozen potato skins. Generally, they can be cooked from frozen and cooked for about 10 to 15 minutes at 200°C, 400°F, Gas mark 6. They can be grilled as well.

Wash, dry and chop the chives. Put the sour cream in the bowl. Add the chives. Stir round. Serve with the hot potato skins.

ADDITIONS & ALTERNATIVES
Try with other dressings like Guacamole (page 270) or Fresh Mexican Salsa (see page 276).

FRESH MEXICAN SALSA

Enough for a large packet of taco chips   ① *Preparation 5 min*
– Moderate

INGREDIENTS
1 green pepper
Bunch coriander
1 or 2 green chillies or $\frac{1}{2}$ teaspoon chilli powder
1 medium onion
Clove garlic
1 large ripe tomato
Pinch salt
1 teaspoon sugar

EQUIPMENT
Sharp knife
Chopping board
Set of measuring spoons
Food processor liquidiser (optional)

METHOD
Wash the green pepper. Take the seeds out. Wash the coriander and cut off the stalks. Carefully take the seeds out of the chillies. Peel the onion and the garlic. Put all the ingredients in a food processor or liquidiser and blend together for about 10 seconds.

If no food processor, chop everything up really small then mix in a bowl.

ADDITIONS & ALTERNATIVES
Serve with tortilla chips, or with enchiladas, tacos or tortillas.

FRESH CHILLI – A WARNING! When you chop up the chillies be careful and avoid getting juice on your hands. It will sting. If you touch your eyes, mouth or other sensitive areas even an hour after chopping them they will smart and burn. So wash your hands or wear rubber gloves.

CHEESE SALSA

Enough for a large packet　　　　① *Preparation 2 min – Easy*
of tortillo chips

INGREDIENTS

Half a 300 g jar Taco relish, or ½ quantity Fresh Mexican Salsa
　(recipe above)
200 g pack processed cheese spread
1 small carton (142 ml or 5 fl oz) sour cream

EQUIPMENT

Spoon
Bowl

METHOD

Mix all the ingredients together.

ADDITIONS & ALTERNATIVES

Use chopped vegetables like carrot, cauliflower or celery to dip in
the salsa.

Use as an accompaniment to burgers or ribs.

REFRIED BEANS

Serves 2 to 4   ⏱ *Preparation 2 min, Cooking 10 min – Easy*

INGREDIENTS
420 g tin baked beans
440 g red kidney beans
1 tablespoon butter
$\frac{1}{2}$ teaspoon paprika pepper
$\frac{1}{2}$ teaspoon chilli powder

EQUIPMENT
Tin opener
Set of measuring spoons
Saucepan
Wooden spoon

METHOD
Open the tins. Drain the kidney beans.

Put the butter, paprika and chilli powder in the pan. Put on a low heat and melt the butter. Add the baked beans and red kidney beans. Cook over a low heat for 5 minutes. Leave to cool.

Can be reheated later or eaten immediately.

ADDITIONS & ALTERNATIVES
You can add some grated Cheddar cheese.

Serve with green salad or with other Tex-Mex dishes.

CHILLI CON CARNE

Serves 2–3   ① *Preparation 5 min, Cooking 45 min – Easy*

INGREDIENTS

100 g (4 oz) mushrooms (about 10) (optional)
1 large onion
2 tablespoons oil
500 g (1 lb) mince
1 packet Mexican chilli seasoning
1 teaspoon salt
400 g tin plum tomatoes
440 g tin red kidney beans

EQUIPMENT

Sharp knife
Chopping board
Set of measuring spoons
Frying-pan
Wooden spoon
Tin opener

METHOD

If using mushrooms, wipe the dirt off and cut the end off the stalk. Slice roughly. Peel and chop the onion.

Put the oil in the frying-pan. Fry the onion over a medium heat for a couple of minutes to soften, stirring to stop it sticking. Add the mince and continue to fry, breaking up the meat with the spoon so that it browns. This should take about five minutes. Add the seasoning and salt and mix well.

Open the tin of tomatoes. Pour in the juice from the tin and then mash up the tomatoes in the tin with a wooden spoon. Add the mashed up tomatoes. Stir and bring to the boil. Turn down the heat so the mixture is just boiling.

Open the tin of kidney beans and drain off the liquid. Add the beans to the pan. Add the mushrooms. Stir from time to time. If it looks like it is getting too dry then add some water. Cook for at least 15 minutes.

You can let it cool and reheat when the rice is done. It seems that the flavour improves with reheating.

ADDITIONS & ALTERNATIVES

Serve this with boiled rice, American long grain being the best for this. Look at the packet to see how long to cook it. There are full instructions on boiled rice in the 'How to' chapter.

Read what it says on the packet of seasoning to get the right amount. Try substituting half to one teaspoon chilli powder and 2 teaspoons ground cumin for the seasoning mix.

Leave out the onions and mushrooms.

Try adding a small tin of sweet corn.

Add 1 chopped sweet pepper.

It's easy to double up the quantities.

MEXICAN CHICKEN TORTILLAS

Makes enough for 8 tortillas ⏱ *Preparation 10 min, Cooking 15 min – Easy*

INGREDIENTS

100 g (4 oz) grated Cheddar cheese (about 2 cups)
Iceberg or other crisp lettuce
2 large ripe tomatoes
500 g frozen small chicken breasts or chicken breasts chopped into bite-sized pieces
1 red pepper
1 large onion
3 cloves garlic
2 tablespoons oil
1 teaspoon ground cumin
1 teaspoon paprika pepper
1 teaspoon chilli pepper
1 pack ready made soft tortillas
300 g jar taco salsa or Mexican Salsa on page 276

EQUIPMENT

Set of measuring cups
Grater
3 small bowls or plates
Sharp knife
Chopping board
Set of measuring spoons
Frying-pan
Wooden spoon

METHOD

Grate the cheese and put in a bowl. Wash and drain the lettuce. Shred it and put in a bowl. Chop the tomatoes into 1 cm (half-inch) chunks. Put them in the last bowl.

Make sure the chicken is defrosted (follow the instructions on the pack), but at least 6 hours at room temperature. Chop the chicken into bite-sized bits.

Wash and chop the red pepper. Discard the central white lump and the seeds. Peel and chop the onion and garlic.

Put the oil in the frying pan. Heat the oil over a medium heat. Add the onion and garlic and fry for a couple of minutes to soften them up. Add the ground cumin, paprika and chilli. Stir round. Add the chicken and cook for five minutes, stirring to make sure the chicken is cooked on all sides. Add the sweet pepper and stir and cook for two minutes. Add two tablespoons of water. Stir round. Cook for three minutes.

Warm the tortillas either by putting under a grill for 10 seconds each or by putting in a warm oven for a couple of minutes. Look at packet for details.

This is a simple construction job. Put a tablespoon or so of the cooked chicken mix on the tortilla, add shredded lettuce, chopped tomato and grated cheese with salsa. Fold up the tortilla and eat with your hands.

ADDITIONS & ALTERNATIVES

You can use Chilli con Carne (page 279) or taco meat mixture (page 286) instead of the chicken.

ENCHILADA SAUCE

Enough for 8 tortillas ① *Preparation 3 min, Cooking 5 min – Easy*

INGREDIENTS
2 tablespoons sunflower oil
1 clove garlic
1 medium onion
1 teaspoon cumin powder
1 teaspoon chilli powder
1 teaspoon paprika
Half 500 g carton creamed tomato
Salt and freshly ground pepper to taste

EQUIPMENT
Set of measuring spoons
Frying-pan
Garlic crusher
Sharp knife
Chopping board
Wooden spoon

METHOD
Put the oil in the frying-pan. Peel and crush the garlic into the pan. Peel and chop the onion. Fry the garlic and onion for a couple of minutes till golden. Add the cumin, chilli and paprika and stir round for 30 seconds. Add the tomato. Season with salt and pepper. Bring to the boil. Take off the heat.

ADDITIONS & ALTERNATIVES
You can buy jars of enchilada sauce.

Garlic purée is available in tubes and jars. It keeps for six weeks in the fridge. Check the pack for equivalent amounts.

283

CHEESE ENCHILADAS

Serves 4   ① *Preparation 10 min, Cooking 25 min – Easy*

INGREDIENTS
1 large onion
2 cups grated Mozzarella cheese
1 packet 8 flour tortillas
1 jar enchilada sauce (250 g) or recipe on previous page
1 medium carton (284 ml 10 fl oz) sour cream
Salt and freshly ground pepper

EQUIPMENT
Sharp knife
Chopping board
Grater
Set of measuring cups
Bowl
Ovenproof dish

METHOD
The filling is equal parts of cheese and onion. Peel and chop the onion finely. Chop or grate the cheese. Keep a bit of the cheese to sprinkle on the top. Mix the onion and cheese together in the bowl.

Get a tortilla. Put an eighth of the mixture on the tortilla. Roll it up like a pancake. Put it in an ovenproof baking dish. Repeat for the other seven tortillas. Pour the enchilada sauce over the top. Sprinkle the top with cheese and season with salt and pepper.

Cook in a preheated oven at 180°C, 350°F, Gas mark 4 for 25 minutes. Put a tablespoon of sour cream on each enchilada when serving.

ADDITIONS & ALTERNATIVES

Serve with sour cream, guacamole (page 270), and a bit of salad.

Instead of the cheese filling use Chilli con Carne (page 279), or the Chicken Tortilla filling (page 281).

Substitute Cheddar cheese for the Mozzarella.

Supermarkets sell bags of grated cheese.

NACHOS

Serves 2   ① *Preparation 3 min, Cooking 5 min – Easy*

INGREDIENTS
Half bunch (4–6) spring onions
100 g (4 oz) Cheddar cheese (2 cups)
1 bag (200 g or 8 oz) tortilla chips
300 g jar taco relish, or ½ quantity Fresh Mexican Salsa (page 276)

EQUIPMENT
Sharp knife
Chopping board
Grater for the cheese
Set of measuring cups
Ovenproof dish

METHOD
Clean and prepare the spring onions. Cut the root end off, trim the leaves. Peel off and discard any dried up or slimy leaves. Chop roughly. Grate the cheese.

Put the tortilla chips in the ovenproof dish. Sprinkle with spring onions and cheese. Cook in an oven at 180°C, 350°F, Gas mark 4 for 5 minutes, till the cheese is runny. Take out and pour the relish on top.

ADDITIONS & ALTERNATIVES
Serve with sour cream, guacamole (page 270) and salad.

TACOS

Serves 2–3   ① *Preparation 5 min, Cooking 20 min – Easy*

INGREDIENTS
100 g (4 oz) grated Cheddar cheese (2 cups)
Iceberg or other crisp lettuce
2 large ripe tomatoes
500 g (1 lb) mince
1 packet Mexican taco seasoning
1 packet of 12 taco shells
300 g jar taco salsa or Mexican Salsa (page 276)

EQUIPMENT
Grater
Set of measuring cups
3 bowls
Sharp knife
Chopping board
Frying-pan
Wooden spoon

METHOD
Grate the cheese and put in a bowl. Wash and drain the lettuce.
Shred it and put in a bowl. Chop the tomatoes into 1 cm (half-inch)
chunks. Put them in the last bowl.

Add the mince to the frying-pan on a medium heat, and fry,
breaking up the meat with the spoon so that it browns. This should
take about five minutes. Add the seasoning mix and stir round.
Add half a cup (quarter pint) of water. Cook on a medium heat till
the fluid is reduced, about 15 minutes.

Warm the taco shells according to the instructions on the packet.

This dish is a construction job. Put two tablespoons or so of the cooked meat mix in the taco, add shredded lettuce, chopped tomato and grated cheese with salsa. Eat with your hands.

ADDITIONS & ALTERNATIVES

Read what it says on the packet of seasoning to get the right amount. Try substituting half to one teaspoon chilli powder and 2 teaspoons ground cumin for the seasoning mix.

Try adding a small tin of sweet corn to the meat mixture as it is cooking.

Add 1 chopped sweet pepper to the meat mixture.

HAMBURGERS

4 quarter pounders ① Preparation 10 min, Cooking 10 min – Easy

INGREDIENTS
Lettuce leaves
1 large (beef) tomato
1 large onion (optional)
4 burger buns
500 g (1 lb) chuck steak or minced steak
2 tablespoons mayonnaise (optional)
Relishes
Ketchup
Salt and freshly ground pepper to taste

EQUIPMENT
Sharp knife
Chopping board
Food processor or mincer, or friendly butcher if mincing specially
Set of measuring spoons
Hamburger patty press (optional)

METHOD
Wash and drain the lettuce. Wash and slice the tomato. Peel and slice the onion. Separate the burger bun halves and grill them.

Grind up the meat if not already minced. Put a quarter of it in the hamburger press and push. Take out and repeat for each one.

If you don't have a hamburger press, you will have to use something to bind the meat together. Put the mince in a bowl with an egg and beat round. If it looks too wet add a tablespoon of breadcrumbs. Then use your hands to press the mixture into flat disks. Make them fairly chunky.

Grill the burgers for about 5 minutes a side. If the meat was very lean (had no fat) put a teaspoon of butter on each burger.

Get the bun. If you like put some mayonnaise on the bottom half. Then put some lettuce leaves on the bun, followed by the onion, burger, tomato and top of the bun.

Serve with the relish and ketchup.

ADDITIONS & ALTERNATIVES

Serve with a bit more salad or oven chips.

To make the meat go further peel and grate and add 1 medium carrot.

Vegetarian version. Buy vegetarian burgers. Some supermarkets sometimes make their own. Go for ones that say 'chargrilled' as they taste better.

TIPS

You can use mince for this, but grinding chuck steak is much better. You know what you're getting. Chuck steak is a cut of beef, with not too much fat, and reasonably cheap. Any steak type can be ground up into mince. The cheaper the mince the more fat and the less 'meat'.

The hamburger press is a steel contraption which you fill with minced meat and press. It gives uniform size and thickness to your burgers. Handmade burgers tend to fall apart, and have thin edges which cook too quickly.

INDIAN

APPLE & TAMARIND SAMBAL

A fresh chutney   ⏱ *Preparation 10 min – Easy*

INGREDIENTS
Half a pack tamarind
2 cups water
1 medium cooking apple
$\frac{1}{2}$ teaspoon ground pepper
$\frac{1}{2}$ teaspoon chilli powder
2 teaspoons sugar

EQUIPMENT
Bowl
Set of measuring cups
Vegetable peeler
Apple corer
Grater
Set of measuring spoons

METHOD
Break up the tamarind and put in the bowl with the water. Squeeze the tamarind so the flesh comes away from the pips. Mush it all up. Throw away the pulp and keep the water.

Peel the apple, take the core out. Grate up the apple. Put in the

bowl with the tamarind water, pepper, chilli and sugar.
That's all there is to it.

ADDITIONS & ALTERNATIVES
Dried tamarind comes in blocks with seeds or tubs without.

CUCUMBER, ONION OR MINT RAITA

Eat with curry   ① *Preparation 3 min – Easy*

INGREDIENTS
250 g set, natural yoghurt
one of the following:
$\frac{1}{4}$ cucumber
1 small onion
1 teaspoon mint sauce

EQUIPMENT
Bowl
Fork
Sharp knife
Chopping board
Set of measuring spoons

METHOD
Put the yoghurt in the bowl. Whip it up with a fork. It should go creamy in about ten seconds. Peel the cucumber, if using, and cut into small cubes, about 5 mm (quarter inch). Mix together.

ADDITIONS & ALTERNATIVES
Substitute a small onion, peeled and diced, for the cucumber.
Substitute or add a teaspoon of mint sauce.

PLAIN RICE

Serves 2 or 3　　　① *Preparation 1 min, Cooking 10–15 min – Easy*

INGREDIENTS
1 cup basmati or long grain rice
2 cups of water
$\frac{1}{2}$ teaspoon of salt

EQUIPMENT
Saucepan with lid
Set of measuring cups

METHOD
Read the packet to get the correct cooking time. Put the water and the rice in the saucepan with the salt. Bring to the boil. Turn down the heat to low. Stir once to stop it sticking to the pan. Put the lid on the pan. Cook for the correct time until the fluid is absorbed (10–15 minutes for long grain or basmati rice). Do not stir until the time is up.

Leave it to stand for a couple of minutes. Free up the grains of rice by flicking with a fork.

ADDITIONS & ALTERNATIVES
The cup referred to is a standard measuring cup of 250 ml. It is approximately the same as a mug.

Generally use twice as much water as rice.

Brown rice takes longer to cook. Read the packet.

Basmati is more fragrant than long grain, and also more forgiving, because it holds together well.

TANDOORI QUICK FRY

Serves 2   ① *Preparation 5 min, Cooking 15 min – Easy*

INGREDIENTS
2 boneless chicken breasts
2 tablespoons sunflower oil
1 tablespoon lemon or lime juice
4 tablespoons Tandoori powder
1 large onion
2 tablespoons sunflower oil for frying
4 cloves garlic

EQUIPMENT
Sharp knife
Chopping board
Set of measuring spoons
Bowl
Frying-pan
Garlic crusher
Wooden spoon

DEFROSTING
Make sure frozen chicken is completely thawed before use. This means leaving it in the fridge overnight, or out of the fridge, covered, for six hours.

METHOD
Cut the chicken into bite-sized pieces.

Put the oil, lemon or lime juice and the Tandoori powder in the bowl. Mix. Add the chicken and stir to coat with the mixture. Leave to stand for anything between 30 minutes and 24 hours in a fridge.

Peel and chop the onion. Put the oil in the frying-pan and heat over a moderate heat. Peel and crush the garlic into the pan. Fry

293

the onion for about three minutes till it is golden, stirring to stop it sticking. Add the chicken and fry till chicken is done, about 10 minutes.

ADDITIONS & ALTERNATIVES

Serve with chutney, naan bread and rice.

Substitute other boneless chicken bits.

COURGETTE & CUMIN

Serves 2–4 as side dish⊕ Preparation 2 min, Cooking 5 min – Easy

INGREDIENTS

3 courgettes
2 tablespoons butter
1 to 2 teaspoons cumin seed

EQUIPMENT

Sharp knife
Chopping board
Set of measuring spoons
Frying-pan
Wooden spoon

METHOD

Wash the courgettes. Cut off the top and bottom ends. Slice lengthways. The slices should be about half a centimetre (quarter inch) thick.

Put the butter and the cumin seed in the frying-pan. Put on a medium heat and melt the butter. Gently fry the courgettes for about five minutes, turning occasionally.

TIPS

Makes a good accompaniment to other curries.

TANDOORI CHICKEN

Serves 4   ① *Preparation 15 min, Cooking 45 min – Easy*

INGREDIENTS
4 large chicken quarters or 8–12 pieces
2 medium onions
2 cloves garlic
3 tablespoons Greek unsweetened yoghurt
4 tablespoons Tandoori mix (check amount on pack)
1 lemon

EQUIPMENT
Sharp knife
Chopping board
Set of measuring spoons
Bowl
Wooden spoon
Casserole, roasting dish or Tandoori pot
Aluminium foil if the dish has no lid

DEFROSTING
Make sure frozen chicken is completely thawed before use. This means leaving it in the fridge overnight, or out of the fridge, covered, for six hours.

METHOD
Peel and chop the onion and garlic. Mix the yoghurt, Tandoori mix, onion and garlic in the bowl.

Slash the chicken pieces through to the bone on the legs, thighs and breast. Rub the Tandoori mix over the chicken pieces so it is well coated. Leave for at least an hour to soak in. It is better to leave it for twelve to twenty-four hours.

Put the chicken in the casserole, roasting dish or Tandoori oven. Put a lid on, or cover the top in aluminium foil. Cook in a preheated oven for 200°C, 400°F, Gas mark 6 for about 35 minutes. Take off the lid or foil, turn the chicken bits over and cook for another ten minutes or so till it is golden and cooked through.

Chicken is cooked if the juices run clear when it is pierced by a fork.

Cut the lemon into quarters and serve with the chicken.

ADDITIONS & ALTERNATIVES
Serve with rice, salad, naan bread.

TIPS
Prepared garlic is sold in tubes and jars. Just read the tube or jar for the suggested equivalent amount. It keeps for six weeks in the fridge.

CHICKEN TIKKA

Serves 2 or 3 ① *Preparation 10 min, Cooking 20 min – Easy*

INGREDIENTS
750 g (1½ lbs) boneless chicken pieces
3 tablespoons Tikka mix
3 tablespoons Greek unsweetened yoghurt
2 tablespoons lemon or lime juice, or juice of a lemon or lime
2 or 3 tablespoons sunflower oil

EQUIPMENT
Sharp knife
Chopping board
Set of measuring spoons
Wooden spoon
Bowl

Bamboo skewers
Grill

DEFROSTING

Make sure frozen chicken is completely thawed before use. This means leaving it in the fridge overnight, or out of the fridge, covered, for six hours.

METHOD

Cut chicken into 2 cm (1 inch) chunks. Combine the Tikka mix with the lemon and oil in the bowl and then add the yoghurt. Add the chicken pieces and stir round. Leave covered preferably in a fridge for at least an hour.

Thread the chicken on the skewers, about four or five chunks each. This is a slippery but satisfying job. Grill for 15 to 20 minutes, turning frequently so all sides get cooked.

ADDITIONS & ALTERNATIVES

Serve with salad, naan bread or boiled rice.

CHICKEN TIKKA MASSALA

Serves 2   ① *Preparation 15 min, Cooking 25 min – Easy*

INGREDIENTS

750 g (1½ lbs) boneless chicken pieces
3 tablespoons Tikka mix
3 tablespoons Greek unsweetened yoghurt
2 tablespoons lemon or lime juice, or juice of a lemon or lime
2 tablespoons sunflower oil
For sauce
3 tablespoons of chopped fresh coriander
200 ml (½ pint) single cream
1 tablespoon Tikka Mix

EQUIPMENT
Sharp knife
Chopping board
Set of measuring spoons
Bowl
Wooden spoon
Bamboo skewers
Grill
Frying-pan

DEFROSTING
Make sure frozen chicken is completely thawed before use. This means leaving it in the fridge overnight, or out of the fridge, covered, for six hours.

METHOD
Cut chicken into 2 cm (1 inch) chunks. Combine the Tikka mix with the lemon and oil in the bowl and then add the yoghurt. Add the chicken pieces and stir. Leave covered preferably in a fridge for at least an hour.

Thread the chicken on the skewers, about four or five chunks each. This is a slippery but satisfying job. Grill for 15 to 20 minutes, turning frequently so all sides get cooked.

Pick the dead leaves off the coriander. Wash and chop the leaves and throw away the stalks. Put the cream, Tikka mix and half the coriander in the frying-pan. Warm up. Take the chicken off the bamboo skewers, and put in the frying-pan. Stir round. Just before serving, sprinkle the rest of the coriander on top.

ADDITIONS & ALTERNATIVES
Serve with salad, naan bread or boiled rice.

Use firm white fish (cod, hake, haddock) instead of the chicken. It works well.

BELPOORI

Serves 4 to 6   ① *Preparation 10 min, Cooking 15 min*
                         – Easy curry accompaniment

INGREDIENTS
2 cold boiled medium-sized potatoes
2 tablespoons fresh coriander
1 medium onion
1 or 2 tablespoons oil
2 or 3 puffed rice wafers or 1 cup of puffed rice
Half a packet of 'Punjab Pooris'
1 teaspoon tamarind paste

EQUIPMENT
Sharp knife
Chopping board
Saucepan
Bowl
Wooden spoon
Set of measuring spoons
Cup

METHOD
If you need to cook the potatoes, new ones are best. Peel the potatoes, cutting away any nasty bits, and cutting out any eyes. Chop the potatoes into quarters. Cook for 10 to 15 minutes in boiling water till just cooked. Drain and allow to cool. Cut into small pieces.

Wash, drain and chop the coriander leaves. Peel and chop the onion. Put the oil in the bowl with the potato, onion and coriander. Stir round. All this can be made in advance.

Break the puffed rice wafers into individual bits of puffed rice. Add the puffed rice to the bowl and stir round. Put a couple of tablespoons of the potato mixture on to plates. Break up the Pooris, or eat the whole ones and use the bits. Sprinkle some broken pooris on top. Mix the teaspoon of tamarind paste in a cup of cold water. Add a tablespoon of tamarind water and serve.

TIPS
Tamarind paste comes from Indian supermarkets or some larger supermarkets stock it.

HOT CHICKEN JALFREZI

Serves 4   ⏱ *Preparation 5 min, Cooking 25 min – Easy*

INGREDIENTS
500 g (1 lb) chicken
1 large onion
1 tablespoon of oil
3 tablespoons Hot Curry Paste
1 small tin tomatoes (about 200 g)
1 red pepper
1 green pepper

EQUIPMENT
Sharp knife
Chopping board
Saucepan with lid
Wooden spoon
Set of measuring spoons
Tin opener

DEFROSTING
Make sure frozen chicken is completely thawed before use. This means leaving it in the fridge overnight, or out of the fridge, covered, for six hours.

METHOD

Cut chicken into 2 cm (1 inch) chunks. Peel and chop the onion. Put the oil in the saucepan and fry the onion for about three minutes till it is golden, stirring to stop it sticking. Add the chicken. Fry and stir for a couple of minutes. Add the curry paste. Stir and fry for another couple of minutes. Add the tomatoes. Stir. Bring to the boil, then turn the heat down so it is just boiling (simmering). Put a lid on the pan and cook for about 20 minutes. Stir a couple of times. If it gets too dry add a bit of water (a couple of tablespoons).

Meanwhile, wash the red and green peppers. Cut the top bits off and remove the seeds. Slice up. Add the peppers about half-way through the cooking.

ADDITIONS & ALTERNATIVES

Serve with rice.

Use 2 tablespoons of hot curry powder instead of the Hot Curry Paste.

ROGAN JOSH, A MEDIUM CURRY

Serves 4   ① *Preparation 10 min, Cooking 2½ hours – Easy*

INGREDIENTS

500 g (1 lb) boneless lamb
1 large onion
1 tablespoon sunflower oil
1 sachet Rogan Josh curry powder
400 g tin of tomatoes

EQUIPMENT

Sharp knife
Chopping board

Set of measuring spoons
Saucepan
Casserole with lid
Wooden spoon
Tin opener

METHOD

The lamb should be lean, that is not have too much fat on it. Chops are therefore not a good idea.

Cut the lamb in cubes. Peel and chop the onion. Put the oil in the saucepan and heat over a moderate heat. Fry the onion for about three minutes till it is golden, stirring to stop it sticking. Fry the lamb for 5 minutes, stirring to keep it from sticking. The outside should be browned. Add the contents of the packet of Rogan Josh curry powder. Stir round. Put the lot in the casserole.

Open the tin of tomatoes. Pour the juice into the casserole. Use the wooden spoon to mash the tomatoes while they are still in the can. Pour the mashed tomatoes into the casserole. Stir it round. Put a lid on the casserole.

Cook in an oven at 180°C, 350°F, Gas mark 4 for 2 hours.

ADDITIONS & ALTERNATIVES

Serve with rice and pickles.

There are full instructions on cooking plain rice on page 292 and pilau rice on page 310.

POTATO & CAULIFLOWER CURRY

Serves 2–4   ① *Preparation 10 min, Cooking 25 min – Easy*

INGREDIENTS

1 medium onion
2 cloves garlic

1 large tomato
4 medium potatoes (about 500 g or 1 lb)
4 tablespoons oil
1 medium cauliflower
1 tablespoon lemon juice
Salt and pepper to taste
1 tablespoon of mild or medium curry powder
or try this mixture instead
1 teaspoon paprika
$\frac{1}{2}$ teaspoon turmeric
$\frac{1}{2}$ teaspoon cumin powder
$\frac{1}{2}$ teaspoon cinnamon
$\frac{1}{2}$ teaspoon chilli powder
$\frac{1}{2}$ teaspoon cardamom powder (optional)
$\frac{1}{2}$ teaspoon clove powder (optional)

EQUIPMENT
Sharp knife
Chopping board
Saucepan
Deep frying-pan, balti dish or wok
Wooden spoon
Set of measuring spoons

METHOD
Peel and chop the onion. Peel and chop the garlic. Chop the tomato. Peel and boil the potatoes for 10 minutes. Drain and chop them into 1 cm (half-inch) cubes.

Heat the oil in the frying-pan. Add the onions and fry for three minuets till golden. Add the garlic and all the spices or the curry powder. Stir round. Add the potatoes and fry for 5 minutes. Stir to stop it sticking and burning. Add the cauliflower and cook and stir for 5 minutes. Add the chopped tomato and lemon. Season with salt and pepper. Cook for 5 minutes.

ADDITIONS & ALTERNATIVES

Serve with rice. There are full instructions on cooking plain rice on page 292 and Pilau rice on page 310.

TIPS

Prepared garlic is sold in tubes and jars. Just read the tube or jar for the suggested equivalent amount. It keeps for six weeks in the fridge.

LAMB KORMA, A MILD CURRY

Serves 4 ① *Preparation 10 min, Cooking 40 min – Easy*

INGREDIENTS

500 g (1 lb) lamb steak
1 large onion
1 tablespoon oil
3 tablespoons mild curry paste
2 tablespoons dried coconut milk powder
3 tablespoons Greek yoghurt

EQUIPMENT

Sharp knife
Chopping board
Saucepan
Wooden spoon
Set of measuring spoons
Set of measuring cups

DEFROSTING

Defrost lamb in a single layer for four hours at room temperature or overnight in the fridge.

METHOD

The lamb should be lean. Chops are therefore not a good idea unless you can hand pick them.

Cut the lamb in cubes. Peel and chop the onion. Put the oil in the saucepan and heat over a moderate heat. Fry the onion for about three minutes till it is golden, stirring to stop it sticking. Add the lamb and fry for 5 minutes, stirring to keep it from sticking. The outside should be browned. Add the mild curry paste and half a cup (120 ml or $\frac{1}{4}$ pint) water.

Mix the coconut milk with a couple of tablespoons of water. Add to the curry. If you add it to the curry directly it may not dissolve property. Bring back to the boil, then turn the heat down so it is just boiling (simmering). Put a lid on the pan and cook for about 30 minutes. Stir a couple of times. If it gets too dry add a bit of water (a couple of tablespoons at a time).

Just before serving stir in the yoghurt.

ADDITIONS & ALTERNATIVES

Serve with plain rice (page 292).

Use 2 tablespoons of mild curry powder instead of the mild curry paste.

MIXED VEGETABLE CURRY

Serves 4   ① *Preparation 10 min, Cooking 25 min – Easy*

INGREDIENTS

2 large potatoes
1 large carrot
1 handful (100g or 4 oz) French beans, runner beans or mange tout
1 courgette

$^{1}_{2}$ cauliflower head
3 tablespoons oil
2 teaspoons cumin
2 teaspoons turmeric
Salt
400 g tin plum tomatoes
$^{1}_{2}$ teaspoon chilli powder

EQUIPMENT
Sharp knife
Chopping board
Large frying-pan or Wok
Set of measuring spoons
Wooden spoon
Tin opener

METHOD
Peel and dice the potatoes. Peel and slice the carrot. Wash all the other vegetables. Break the cauliflower into 1 cm (half-inch) bits. Cut up the other vegetables.

Heat the oil in the frying-pan. Add the potatoes, carrot, cumin, turmeric and salt, and fry for 5 minutes. Stir to stop it sticking and to coat the potato and carrot evenly. Add the tomatoes and chilli powder and stir for a couple of minutes. Add the rest of the vegetables and stir round. Add enough water to cover the vegetables. Bring to the boil and simmer for 15–20 minutes until potatoes are cooked.

ADDITIONS & ALTERNATIVES
Serve with rice.

Use mild curry powder instead of the spices above.

Use any fresh vegetables that are available. Leave out any you find loathsome, increase the amount of any you particularly like.

DAAL

Serves 2 ⏲ *Preparation 5 min, Cooking 30 mins – Easy*

INGREDIENTS
250 g red split lentils, about 1½ cups
1 teaspoon turmeric
1 teaspoon salt
1 large onion
2 cloves garlic
1 tablespoon oil
1 tablespoon garam masala

EQUIPMENT
Saucepan
Set of measuring spoons
Set of measuring cups
Wooden spoon
Sharp knife
Chopping board
Frying-pan

METHOD
Wash the lentils. Put the lentils in the pan with about 500 ml (1 pint) water and the turmeric and salt. Bring to the boil. Turn down the heat so that the water is just boiling (simmering). Stir from time to time. The object is to get the lentils to a smooth paste. This takes about 30 minutes. It may need more water to stop it sticking.

Peel and slice the onion and garlic. Put the oil in the frying-pan. Fry the onion and the garlic until they are caramelised and dark brown.

When the lentils are smooth, stir in the garam masala, put into a bowl and put the onion and garlic on top.

TIPS

Prepared garlic is sold in tubes and jars. Just read the tube or jar for the suggested equivalent amount. It keeps for six weeks in the fridge.

LAMB OR CHICKEN MADRAS

Serves 4   ① *Preparation 5 min, Cooking 55 min – Moderate*
                (you have to keep an eye on it while it is cooking)

INGREDIENTS

1 kg (2 lbs) of lamb steak or chicken pieces
1 large onion
2 cloves garlic
3 tablespoons oil
About 2 tablespoons Madras powder or paste (see below)
400 g tin tomatoes
Salt
1–2 tablespoons lemon juice

EQUIPMENT

Sharp knife
Chopping board
Frying-pan
Set of measuring spoons
Wooden spoon
Tin opener

DEFROSTING

Make sure frozen chicken is completely thawed before use. This means leaving it in the fridge overnight, or out of the fridge, covered, for six hours.

METHOD

Cut the lamb or chicken into 2 cm (1 inch) cubes. Peel and chop the onion and the garlic.

Put the oil in a pan. Cook the onion and garlic, stirring so they don't stick. Add the Madras curry powder. Cook for three minutes. Add the chopped lamb pieces or chicken pieces. Fry for five minutes, stirring. Add the mashed-up tinned tomatoes and juice and some salt to taste. Stir and bring to the boil. Turn down the heat and cook gently, stirring from time to time, till the oil comes to the top and the meat is tender. If it gets too dry add a little water, to make thick gravy. Cook for 45 minutes. Add the lemon juice.

ADDITIONS & ALTERNATIVES

Serve with boiled rice and chutney, and Cucumber, Onion or Mint Raita (see page 291).

There are several brands of Madras powder or paste. The exact quantity of these vary but are in the region of 2 tablespoons per kg (2 lb) of meat. Read the packet. There are also cook-in sauces, both in tins and jars. They are OK as a last resort.

TIPS

Madras curry is fairly hot. Keep to the quantity of any powder suggested on the packet the first time you cook it. If it isn't hot enough either increase the amount of Madras powder or add extra chilli. A BAD mistake is to try the taste before it is cooked and add more chilli. As it cooks it gets hotter.

Prepared garlic is sold in tubes and jars. Just read the tube or jar for the suggested equivalent amount. It keeps for six weeks in the fridge.

PILAU RICE

Serves 4   ① *Preparation 10 min, Cooking 30 min – Moderate*

INGREDIENTS
$\frac{1}{2}$ cup almonds
3 tablespoons sunflower oil
3 cups long grain rice
2 medium onions
1 teaspoon ground turmeric
$\frac{1}{4}$ teaspoon saffron
5 cups chicken stock (or water and stock cubes)
1 teaspoon salt
$\frac{1}{4}$ teaspoon of peppercorns
$\frac{1}{4}$ cup sultanas
1 cup cooked peas

EQUIPMENT
Frying-pan
Set of measuring spoons
Sieve
Sharp knife
Chopping board
Set of measuring cups
Large thick-bottomed saucepan with a lid
Wooden spoon
Fork

METHOD
Fry the almonds gently in 1 tablespoon of oil till golden brown. Take out of the pan. Take the pan off the heat.

Wash and drain the rice. Peel and chop the onions. Heat the rest of the oil, preferably in a thick-bottomed pan. Fry the onions, stirring, until golden brown. Add the turmeric, saffron and rice and stir well. Fry for about five minutes until the rice is golden and coated. Add the stock to the pan and bring to the boil. Add about 1 teaspoon salt and the peppercorns. Stir well. Put a lid on the pan. Turn the heat down so it is just boiling (simmering) and cook for 20 minutes. Don't stir, and if you can handle the stress, don't take the lid off.

Turn off the heat. Take the lid off. Leave to stand for ten minutes, to let the steam out. Loosen the grains with a fork. Add the sultanas, almonds and peas and serve.

ADDITIONS & ALTERNATIVES

Try adding 3 whole cardamom pods and/or a 2 cm (1 inch) cinnamon stick when the stock is added to the rice.

TIKKA BARBECUE

Serves 4   ① *Preparation 5 min, up to a day to stand,*
Cooking 25 min – Easy

INGREDIENTS
8 chicken legs
2 tablespoons oil
1 tablespoon lemon juice (half a lemon)
2 tablespoons Tikka mix powder

EQUIPMENT
Sharp knife
Chopping board
Wooden spoon
Bowl
Set of measuring spoons

METHOD
Slash the chicken legs through to the bone.

Mix the oil, lemon juice and Tikka mix in a bowl. Put the chicken legs in the bowl and stir round till they are covered. It is best to leave this in a fridge overnight, though half an hour will do.

Barbecue or grill for about 25 minutes, turning from time to time.

ADDITIONS & ALTERNATIVES

Serve with French bread and salad.

Use a plastic box with a lid to mix the powder, lemon and oil. Shake it to make sure the legs are covered.

Other chicken bits will do.

SALADS FOR BARBECUES

Recipes for all the following are in the salad chapter. They are all easy, and can be made in quantity. The least trouble and most unusual is the watermelon.

Watermelon & Feta Cheese Salad (page 69)
Greek Salad (page 72)
Coleslaw (page 77)
Chick Pea Salad (page 70)
Pasta Salad (page 79)

MEATS FOR BARBECUES

Burgers (page 288)
Sausages (page 144)
Spare Ribs with Barbecue Sauce (page 273)

FISH FOR BARBECUES

Salmon Steaks wrapped in tin foil
Trout
Sardines

VEGETARIAN OPTIONS

Vegetarian burgers or sausages
Whole Sweet Corn

SAUCES

Fresh Mexican Salsa (page 276)
Barbecue Sauce (page 272)

EASY BULK PARTY FOOD

Make food that is quick and easy.

Recipes for all of the following can be found in the book
Hummus & pitta bread (page 49)
Prawn Dip and crisps (page 47)
Taco chips and Fresh Mexican Salsa (page 276)
Potato Salad (page 82)
Greek Salad (page 72)
Pasta Salad (page 79)
Mini Pizza (page 58)

There are no recipes for the following which require no preparation
French bread and Brie cheese
Grapes
Apples

DRINKS

General

We drink water with most meals. It is also reasonable to offer anyone a non-alcoholic drink, particularly if they are driving. Anyway, a broad exposition on alcohol is well beyond the scope of this book. If you need any instruction, please write to the publishers demanding they commission 'Drinking for Blokes'.

Lager

Lager makes a refreshing drink with curry, Chinese, Italian and Tex-Mex.

Red Wine

Lots of red wines are available. It is traditionally the accompaniment for meat. Some supermarkets are grading wine A to E for how full-bodied they are. A robust Cabernet Sauvignon or Shiraz (Syrah) would be C or D.

Red wine should not be chilled, but served at room temperature.

White Wine

White wine comes from sharp and fruity through creamy or buttery to sweet. It is better served chilled. There are some very good Australian or New Zealand wines. Supermarkets are keen to get your business and often describe the wine well on the label of the bottle.

Some off-licence chains (particularly Oddbins) can be very helpful.

Some supermarkets are grading white wine from 1 (dry) to 6 (sweet). Number 2 is a good place to start with an Australian Chardonay or Semillion. White wine is good with fish and chicken.

Try to avoid the sweetish German wines. Although it is none of our business what you choose to drink, they are probably the most consistently bland and mediocre to poor wines on the market.

Rosé or Rosada

Rosé or Rosada are pink wines. There are several good ones around and a good supermarket or off-licence will know which.

The label often says serve chilled but try it at room temperature, because some have a delicate strawberry or raspberry flavour and chilling kills it dead.

They are thought of as summer wines and are great for picnics or barbecues. They are also good with chicken or salads. They are not very strong so do not go well with highly spiced food like curry.

COLD PUNCH

Serves 15–20   ⏲ *Preparation 5 min – Easy*

INGREDIENTS
1 bunch mint
3 oranges
2 apples
3 lemons
2 litres orange juice
1 litre pineapple juice
1 bottle rum
1 litre fizzy water
1 bag ice

EQUIPMENT
Sharp knife
Chopping board
Juicer for the lemon
Bowl

METHOD
Keep all the ingredients in the fridge till you are ready to make the punch.

Wash and drain the mint. Pull off some leaves. Wash and cut the oranges and apples into slices. Discard the apple core and pips. Extract the juice from the lemon and pour into the bowl. Add the orange juice, fruit, pineapple juice and rum. Stir. Add the mint, fizzy water and ice.

ADDITIONS & ALTERNATIVES
Any carton of fruit juice, such as mango or five fruits can be substituted for the orange or pineapple.

HOT PUNCH OR MULLED WINE

Serves 10   ⏱ *Preparation 10 min, Cooling 10 min – Moderate*

INGREDIENTS
1 whole nutmeg
1 cup sugar
3 sticks cinnamon
3 tablespoons whole cloves
4 lemons
3 oranges
2 bottles red wine

EQUIPMENT
Nutcracker or hammer
Sharp knife
Chopping board
Set of measuring spoons
Set of measuring cups
Large saucepan
Wooden spoon
Sieve
Zester
Juicer
Corkscrew

METHOD
Crush the nutmeg with the nut cracker or hammer – it's easier than it looks. Heat the sugar, nutmeg, cinnamon and cloves in the pan with a cup of water. Boil for about 5 minutes, stirring. Take the pan off the heat. Strain the liquid and throw away the cinnamon, nutmeg and cloves. Put the liquid back in the pan.

Use the zester to take the skin off 2 lemons and 2 oranges. Add to the pan. Extract the juice from the oranges and lemons and add to the pan. Put the pan back on the heat and heat up. Add the two bottles of wine. Heat and serve.

ADDITIONS & ALTERNATIVES
This is a drink that is good from Halloween through New Year to early spring.

Add half a bottle of brandy.

Take it easy.

ALCOHOL FREE PUNCH

Serves 15   *① Preparation 10 min – Easy*

INGREDIENTS
2 litres (3 pints) strong tea
1 cup sugar
6 lemons
Bunch mint
1 litre (2 pints) dry ginger ale
Bag ice

EQUIPMENT
Kettle
Teapot
Sieve
Large bowl
Set of measuring cups
Sharp knife
Juicer

METHOD
Keep all the ingredients in the fridge till needed. Make the tea. Strain out the leaves. Dissolve the sugar in the tea. Allow the tea to cool, and put in the fridge.

Cut the lemons in half and extract the juice. Wash the mint and pull off some leaves.

Just before serving put all the ingredients in the bowl. Stir. Add the ice and serve.

ADDITIONS & ALTERNATIVES
Use lemonade instead of the ginger ale.

Add some, strawberries, washed and cut in half.

This can be made into an alcoholic punch by adding a bottle of vodka or rum.

INDEX

Antipasti, 240
Apple
  & tamarind sambal, 290–1
  baked, 200
  corer, 13
  crumble, 203–4
  fritters, 204–5
  orange & cheese salad, 66
  pie, 212–13
  sauce, 162
  strudel, cheat's, 210–11
Aubergine
  with cheese, 59
  chick pea & tomato stew, 181–2
Avocado
  & bacon toasted sandwich, 53–4
  & garlic sausage salad, 71
  & pasta salad, 80–1
  & prawn, 31–2
  & tuna, 31–2
  guacamole, 270–1
  vinaigrette, 31

Bacon
  & avocado toasted sandwich,
    53–4
  & pasta, 249–50
  & tomato quiche, 98

club sandwich, 55–6
spinach & mushroom salad, 78
Banana
  baked, 199
  custard, 194
  split, 196
Barbecue
  fish for, 313
  meat for, 313
  salads, 313
  sauce, 272
  sauces for, 314
  tikka, 312–13
  vegetarian options for, 314
Bean sprout salad, 67
Beans
  cooking, 22, 27–8
  dried, 27–8
  refried, 278
Beef
  braised, 147–8
  chilli con carne, 279–80
  Cornish pasty, 169–70
  goulash, 163–4
  hamburgers, 288–9
  in beer, 146–7
  mince roll, 167–8
  roast, 157–8

321

shepherd's pie, 153–4
steak
  & kidney, 164–5
  grilled, 170–1
  in cream, 144–5
  stew with wine, 172–3
  teriyaki, 228–9
Belpoori, 299–300
Big breakfast pie, 98–9
Blue cheese dressing, 64–5
Bolognese sauce, 246–7
Borlotti beans *see* Rose coco beans,
  85–6
Bowls, 9
Bread & butter pudding, 221
Bread pudding, 220
Bread & tomato salad, 73
Broccoli, 21
  pasta & chilli, 250–1
Butter beans & tomato, 179–80

Cabbage, 21
Cajun chicken, 100
Cajun salmon, 119
Calzoni
  fish, 268–9
  meat, 266–7
  vegetable, 267–8
Camembert
  fried with cranberry sauce,
    44–5
Carbonara ham pasta sauce, 252–3
Carrots, 20
Casserole dishes, 11
Casserole of chicken with bacon &
  mushrooms, 102–3
Cauliflower, 21
  cheese, 185
Cheddar cheese, walnut, celery &

raisin salad, 68
Cheese
  apple & orange salad, 66
  aubergine with, 59
  blue cheese dressing, 64–5
  boursin
    chicken & bacon, 101–2
    & salmon, 121
  Camembert fried with
    cranberry sauce, 44–5
  Cheddar, walnut, celery &
    raisin salad, 68
  enchiladas, 284–5
  Feta & watermelon salad, 69
  Mozzarella salad, 74
  on toast
    basic, 50
    late, 51–2
    smart, 50–1
  salsa, 277
  sandwich, fried with onion, 53
  sandwich, late toasted, 52
  sauce, 184
Chick pea
  and fish stew, 138–9
  salad, 70
Chicken, 100–117
  boursin & bacon, 101–2
  breasts with lemon, 104
  cajun, 100
  casserole, vegetable, 107–8
  casserole with bacon &
    mushroom, 102
  cider, 105
  club sandwich, 55–6
  coronation, 116–17
  creole, 112–13
  defrosting, 28–9
  hot jalfrezi curry, 300–1

Italian roast, 243–4
lemon, Chinese, 231–2
liver paté, 43–4
Madras curry, 308–9
Mexican tortillas, 281–2
Moroccan, 114–15
pot stew, 106
rice bake, 113
roast, 109–10
satay, 233–4
sweet & sour, 227
tandoori, 295–6
tandoori quick fry, 293–4
Thai curry, 235–7
tikka, 296–7
tikka massala, 297–8
vegetable casserole, 107–8
with lemon, 104
Chilli
con carne, 279–80
meatless, 188–9
Chinese & Far Eastern, 222–39
Chinese
spare ribs, 239
pork & ginger, 229–30
Chips, 20
Chocolate
croissant, cheat's, 56–7
pot, rich, 201
Chopping boards, 7
Cider chicken, 105
pork, 152
Club sandwich, 55–6
Colander, 12
Coleslaw, 77
Corer, apple, 13
Corn on the cob, 22
Cornish pasty, 169–70
Coronation chicken, 116–17

Courgettes
& cumin, 294
& tomato bake, 186
grilled, 242
to cook, 22
Crème fraîche brûlée, 206
Crêpes, savoury salmon, 120
Croissant, chocolate, 56–7
Crumble, apple, 203–4
Curry
chicken Madras, 308–9
chicken tikka, 296–7
chicken tikka massala, 297–8
courgettes & cumin, 294
daal, 307–8
hot chicken jalfrezi, 300–1
lamb korma, 304–5
lamb Madras, 308–9
mixed vegetable, 305–6
potato & cauliflower, 302–4
rogan josh, 301–2
tandoori chicken, 295–6
Thai chicken, 235–7
Custard, banana, 194

Daal, 307–8
Defrosting times, 28–9
Desserts, 194–221
apple
baked, 200
crumble, 203–4
fritters, 204–5
pie, 212–13
strudel, cheat's, 210–11
banana
baked, 199
custard, 194
split, 196
bread & butter pudding, 221

bread pudding, 220
crème fraîche brûlée, 206
fruit
    crèpes, 202
    fools, 198
ice cream sundae, 197
lemon pie, 214–15
mille feuille, 218–19
mince tart, 215–16
oranges, marinaded, 195
quick crème brûlée, 207
rice pudding, 209–10
rich chocolate pot, 201
sherry trifle, 208–9
treacle tart, 217
Dip
    prawn, 47
    tahini cream, 48
Dressing, *see* salad dressing
Dried beans, cooking times,
        27–8

Eggs, 87–99
    Big Breakfast Pie, 98–9
    boiled, 87
    fried, 90
    mayonnaise, 88
    omelette, 91
    omelette, Italian meaty, 92–3
    omelette, Spanish, 93–4
    poached, 94–5
    quiche, bacon & tomato, 98
    quiche, walnut & leek, 96–7
    scrambled, 89
Enchilada
    cheese, 284–5
    sauce, 283

Fish, 118–140

calzoni, 268–9
hot whisky smoked, 45–6
in the pan, 123
kippers, 118
Mediterranean, 139–40
plaice
    stuffed, 135–6
    with wine, 122
prawn
    cocktail, 32–3
    dip, 47
    hot garlic, 125
salmon
    boursin, 121
    cajun, 119
    in pastry, 128–9
    poached, 126
    savoury crèpes, 120
    smoked
        roll, 41
        salad, 35–6
sardines, grilled, 60
sea pie, 130–1
smoked mackerel paté, 35
squid rings in batter, 136–7
stew with chick peas, 138–9
trout
    baked, 127
    & almonds, 124
tuna
    in sauce, 132–3
    in mayonnaise, 30–1
    mayonnaise pasta, 248–9
    rice, 133–4
Focaccia, 261–3
Fritters, apple, 204–5
Fruit
    crèpes, 202
    fools, 198

see also apples, banana, grapefruit, lemon, melon, orange, pineapple

Gammon & pineapple, 141
Garlic
   crusher, 14
   mushrooms, 42–3
   prawns, 125
Garlic sausage & avocado salad, 71
Goat's cheese & rocket salad, 39–40
Goulash, 163–4
Grapefruit, grilled, 39
Grater, 13
Gravy, 111
Greek lamb kleftikos, 148–9
Greek salad, 72
Grilled sardines, 60
Guacamole, 270–1

Ham, Parma & melon, 34
Hamburgers, 288–9
Hot garlic prawns, 125
Hot whisky smoked fish, 45–6
Hummus & pitta bread, 49

Ice-cream sundae, 197
Indian, 290–311
Irish stew, 150–1
Italian, 240–69
   meaty omelette, 92–3
   roast chicken, 243–4
   roast lamb, 244
Italian bread, 261–3

Kebab, lamb, 142
Kippers, 118

Knife sharpeners, 7
Knives, 6
Korma, lamb, 304–5

Lager, 315
Lamb
   defrosting, 28–9
   Greek kleftikos, 148–9
   Irish stew, 150–1
   Italian roast, 244
   kebabs, 142
   korma curry, 304–5
   Madras curry, 308–9
   roast, 159–60
   rogan josh curry, 301–2
   shepherd's pie, 153–4
   stuffed breast of, 166
Lasagne, 257–9
   vegetable, 192–3
Lemon
   chicken, 231–2
   pie, 214–15
   seafood & angel's hair pasta, 255–6
Liver paté, chicken, 43–4

Mackerel, smoked paté, 35
Madras curry, chicken or lamb, 308–9
Mange tout, 22
Marinaded oranges, 195
Mashed potatoes, 174–5
Mayonnaise
   egg, 88
   tuna, 248–9
Measuring spoons and cups, 7–8
Meat, 141–73
Mediterranean fish, 139–40
Melon & Parma ham, 34

Mexican
    cheese enchiladas, 284–5
    cheese salsa, 277
    chicken, tortillas, 281–2
    enchilada sauce, 283
    refried beans, 278
    salsa, 276
    tacos, 286–7
Mille feuille, 218–19
Mince
    roll, 167–8
    tart, 215–16
Mini gourmet pizza, 57–8
Mini pizza, 58
Mixed vegetable curry, 305–6
Moroccan chicken, 114–15
Mozzarella salad, 74
Mulled wine, 318–19
Mushrooms
    garlic, 42–3
    spinach & bacon salad, 78

Nachos, 285–6
Niçoise salad, 75
Noodles, 24

Omelette, 91
    Italian meaty, 92–3
    Spanish, 93–4
Onion, roast, 177–8
Orange
    apple & cheese salad, 66
    marinaded, 195
Ovenproof dish, 11–12
Oven temperatures, 4

Pans
    Frying, 11
    overall advice, 9

sauce, 9–10
Parsnips, roast, 177–8
Parties, 312–14
Pasta
    & avocado salad, 80–81
    & bacon, 249–50
    bolognese sauce, 246–7
    broccoli & chilli, 250–1
    carbonara ham sauce, 252–3
    cooking instructions, 25
    lasagne, 257–9
        vegetable, 192–3
    lemon seafood & angel's hair, 255–6
    salad, 79–80
    tomato sauce, 245–6
    tuna mayonnaise, 248–9
    with pesto, 254
Pastry
    case, to bake, 26–7
    how to roll, 26
Paté
    chicken liver, 43–4
    smoked mackerel, 35
Peas, frozen, to cook, 22
Peas, to cook, 17
Peppers, toasted, roasted, 241
Pesto
    & pasta, 254
    tomatoes stuffed with, 37
Pie
    apple, 212–13
    lemon, 214–15
    potato, 187
    sea, 130–1
    shepherd's, 153–4
    vegetarian
        shepherd's, 190–1
Pilau rice, 310–11

Pizza, 264–5
   mini, 58
   mini gourmet, 57–8
Plaice
   stuffed, 135–6
   with wine, 122
Pork
   & cider, 152
   & ginger, Chinese, 229–30
   apple sauce, 162
   chops with orange sauce, 156–7
   goulash, 163–4
   roast, 161–2
   spare ribs
      Chinese, 239
      Texan barbecue, 273
   stir-fry with black bean sauce,
      222–3
   sweet & sour, 226
Potatoes 18–20, 82, 176–8
   & cauliflower curry, 302–4
   baked, 19, 176
   baked & fillings, 176
   boiled, 18
   chips, 20
   mashed, 18–19, 174–5
   pan fried, 20
   pie, 187
   roast, 19, 177–8
   salad, 82
   skins, bought, 275
   skins, fresh cooked, 274
Prawn
   avocado vinaigrette, 31–2
   cocktail, 32–3
   dip, 47
   hot garlic, 125
Pudding
   bread, 220

   bread & butter, 221
   rice, 209–210
Punch
   alcohol free, 320
   cold, 317
   hot, 318–19

Quiche
   bacon & tomato, 98
   walnut & leek, 96–7
Quick crème brûlée, 207

Raita
   cucumber, mint, onion, 291
Refried beans, 278
Rice
   chicken bake, 113
   cooking times, 23–4
   pilau, 310–11
   plain, 292
   pudding, 209–210
   risotto, 259–60
   special fried, 237–8
   tuna with, 133–4
Rich chocolate pot, 201
Risotto, 259–60
Roast
   beef, 157–8
   chicken, 109–10
      Italian, 243–4
   lamb, 159–60
      Italian, 244
   peppers, 241
   pork, 161–2
   potatoes, 177–8
   potatoes, carrots, parsnips &
      onion, 177–8
Rocket & goat's cheese salad,
     39–40

Rogan josh curry, 301–2
Roll
    mince, 167–8
    smoked salmon, 41
Rose coco salad, 85–6

Salad
    apple, orange & cheese, 66
    avocado & garlic sausage, 71
    bean sprout & yoghurt
        dressing, 67
    bread & tomato, 73
    Cheddar cheese, walnut, celery
        & raisin, 68
    chick pea, 70
    coleslaw, 77
    egg mayonnaise, 88
    for barbecues, 313
    Greek, 72
    herbs, 62
    lettuces, 61–2
    Mozzarella, 74
    Niçoise, 75
    pasta, 79–80
    pasta with avocado, 80–1
    potato, 82
    rocket & goat's cheese, 39–40
    rose coco, 85–6
    smoked salmon, 35–6
    spinach, mushroom & bacon,
        78
    tabbouleh, 83–4
    three bean, 84
    tomatoes, 73
    Waldorf, 76
    watermelon & Feta cheese, 69
Salad dressings
    blue cheese, 64–5
    thousand island, 65

    vinaigrette, 63–4
    yoghurt 67
Salads & Dressings, 61–86
Salmon
    boursin, 121
    cajun, 119
    crêpes, savoury, 120
    in pastry, 128–9
    poached, 126
    smoked
        roll, 41
        salad, 35–6
Sandwich
    bacon & avocado, toasted, 53–4
    club, 55–6
    late toasted cheese, 52
Sardines, grilled, 60
Satay chicken, 233–4
Sauce
    apple, 162
    apple & tamarind Indian,
        290–1
    barbecue, 272
    bolognese, 246–7
    carbonara ham, 252–3
    cheese, 184
    cheese salsa, 277
    enchilada, 283
    fresh Mexican salsa, 276
    sweet & sour, 226
    tomato, 245–6
    white, 183
Saucepans, 9–11
Sausages, 143
    toad in the hole, 155
    vegetarian & fried onions, 175
Scrambled egg, 89
Sea pie, 130–1
Shepherd's pie, 153–4

vegetarian, 190–1
Sherry trifle, 208–9
Sieve, 12
Smoked fish, hot, whisky, 45–6
Smoked salmon
    roll, 41
    salad, 35–6
Snacks (*see also* Starters), 47–60
Spanish omelette, 93–4
Spare ribs
    Chinese, 239
    Texan barbecue, 273
Special fried rice, 237–8
Spinach, 21
    mushroom & bacon salad, 78
Squid rings in batter, 136–7
Starters, 30–46
Steak
    & kidney, 164–5
    grilled, 170–1
    in cream, 144–5
Stir-fry
    port with black bean sauce,
        222–3
    vegetables, 224 5
Stuffed
    breast of lamb, 166
    plaice, 135–6
    tomato, 178–9
Sweet & sour chicken, 227
Sweet & sour sauce, 226
Sweet corn, frozen, 17

Tabbouleh, 83–4
Tacos, 286–7
Tahini cream dip, 48
Tandoori
    chicken, 295–6
    quick fry, 293–4

Tart
    mince, 215–16
    treacle, 217
Teriyaki beef, 228–9
Tex-Mex, 270–89
Texan barbecued spare ribs, 273
Thai chicken curry, 235–7
Thousand Island dressing, 65
Three bean salad, 84
Tikka
    barbecue, 312–13
    chicken, 296–7
    chicken massala, 297–8
Toad in the hole, 155
Tomatoes
    & bread salad, 73
    & butter beans, 179–80
    sauce, 245–6
    stuffed, 178–9
    stuffed with pesto, 37
    with spiced filling, 38
Tortillas, Mexican chicken, 281–2
Treacle tart, 217
Trifle, sherry, 208–9
Trout
    & almonds, 124
    baked, 127
Tuna
    avocado vinaigrette, 31–2
    in sauce, 132–3
    mayonnaise, 30–1
    mayonnaise pasta, 248–9
    rice, 133–4

Vegetable lasagne, 192–3
Vegetables
    calzoni, 266–9
    curry, 305–6
    frozen, 17

how to cook, 18–22
stir-fry, 224–5
see also aubergine, beans,
    broccoli, cabbage, carrots,
    cauliflower, corn on the
    cob, courgettes,
    mushrooms, onion,
    parsnips, peas, peppers,
    potatoes, spinach,
    tomatoes
Vegetarian, 174–93
Vinaigrette, 63–4

Waldorf salad, 76
Walnut & leek quiche, 96–7
Watermelon & Feta cheese salad,
    69
Whisky smoked fish, hot, 45–6
White sauce, 183
Wine
    mulled, 318–19
    red, 315
    Rosé, 316
    white, 316
Wok, 14
Wooden spoons, 8